Collins

Weather
ALMANAC

A GUIDE TO
2025

Storm Dunlop & Zoë Johnson

Published by Collins
An imprint of HarperCollins Publishers
Westerhill Road
Bishopbriggs
Glasgow G64 2QT
www.harpercollins.co.uk

HarperCollins Publishers
Macken House
39/40 Mayor Street Upper, Dublin 1
D01 C9W8 Ireland

© HarperCollins Publishers 2024
Text and illustrations © Storm Dunlop, Zoë Johnson and Wil Tirion
Cover illustrations © Julia Murray
Images and illustrations see acknowledgements page 266

The contents of this publication are believed correct at the time of printing.
Nevertheless the publisher can accept no responsibility for errors or omissions,
changes in the detail given or for any expense or loss thereby caused.

HarperCollins does not warrant that any website mentioned in this title will
be provided uninterrupted, that any website will be error free, that defects will
be corrected, or that the website or the server that makes it available are free
of viruses or bugs. For full terms and conditions please refer to the site
terms provided on the website.

A catalogue record for this book is available from the British Library

ISBN 978-0-00-868812-7
10 9 8 7 6 5 4 3 2 1

Printed in the UK using 100% Renewable Electricity at
CPI Group (UK) Ltd

If you would like to comment on any aspect of this book,
please contact us at the above address or online.
e-mail: collins.reference@harpercollins.co.uk

This book contains FSC™ certified paper and other controlled
sources to ensure responsible forest management.

For more information visit: www.harpercollins.co.uk/green

Contents

Introduction

Our variable weather

Anyone living in the British Isles hardly needs to be told that the weather is extremely variable. Rain, wind, snow and sun arrive and disappear from one day – or hour – to the next. Despite what politicians and the media may say, the dramatic weather sometimes experienced in Britain is not 'unprecedented'. Britain has always experienced extreme windstorms, snowfall, rainfall, thunderstorms, flooding and such major events. Even those 'not within living memory of the oldest inhabitant' will have occurred sometime before. What is changing, however, is the frequency of such events. The year 2023 was an exceptional one around the world, with droughts, floods, wildfires and major storms aplenty. It followed record-breaking temperatures in 2022. A recent Met Office report showed that the ten hottest years on record in the UK have all happened since 2002, and six of the ten wettest years on record have occurred since 1998. That is not to say that any meteorologist can look at a specific event or extreme drought and say it was 'caused by climate change' – but the long-term analysis shows an unmistakeable trend of rising temperatures and increases in certain associated weather phenomena. The study of our weather has therefore never been more critical.

The British climate is basically a maritime one, determined by the proximity of these islands to the Atlantic Ocean. Our weather is largely determined by the changes resulting from incursions of dry continental air from the Eurasian landmass to the east, contrasting with the prevailing moist maritime air from the Atlantic Ocean to the west. The general mildness of the climate, in comparison with other locations at a similar latitude, has often been ascribed to the 'Gulf Stream'. In fact, the Gulf Stream exists only on the western side of the Atlantic, along the East Coast of America and the warm current off the coast of Britain is correctly known as the North Atlantic Drift. This warm current is a factor in British weather, but it is not solely the oceanic waters that create our mild climate.

The Rocky Mountains in North America impede the westerly flow of air and create a series of north/south waves that propagate eastwards (and actually right round the world). These waves cause north/south oscillations of the jet stream (which, in our case, is the 'Polar Front' jet stream) that, in turn, controls the progression of the low-pressure areas (the depressions) that travel from west to east and create most of the changeable weather over Britain. The jet stream 'steers' the depressions, sometimes to the north of the British Isles and sometimes far to the south. It may also assume a strong flow in longitude (known as a 'meridional' flow) leading to a blocking situation, where depressions cannot move eastwards and may come to a halt or be forced to travel far to the north or south. Such a block (especially in winter) may draw frigid air directly from the Arctic Ocean or continental air from the east; such air is usually described as 'from Siberia', because it often originates from that region. More rarely, such blocks draw warmer air from the Mediterranean over the country.

The longer-term location of the jet stream itself is governed by something known to meteorologists as the North Atlantic Oscillation (NAO). Basically, this may be thought of as the distribution of pressure between the Azores High over the central Atlantic and the Icelandic Low. These are semi-permanent features of the flow of air around the globe, and are known to meteorologists as 'centres of action'. When the NAO has a 'positive' index, with high pressure and warm air in the south compared with low pressure and low temperatures in the north, depressions are steered north of the British Isles. Although most of the country experiences windy and wet weather, the west and north tends to be affected most, with southern and eastern England warmer and drier. When the NAO has a 'negative' index, the Azores High is displaced towards the north and the jet stream tends to show strong meanders towards the south. Frequently there is a slowly moving low pressure area over the near (north-western) Continent or over the north-eastern Atlantic. The jet stream wraps around this, before turning back to the north. Blocks are, however, most frequent in the spring.

Climatic regions of the British Isles

Although the weather across Britain is always changeable, there are certain characteristic areas of the country that can be associated with particular weather trends. The average route of the jet stream is to the north of the British Isles, allowing the strong westerlies that prevail at these latitudes to bring fronts to our western shores. Additionally, the pressure gradient from the Azores High to the Icelandic Low means northern regions of the British Isles tend to be subjected more often to the depressions arriving from the Atlantic. So overall, the climate of the British Isles may be described as: warmer and drier in the south and east, wetter in the west and north. Details of the weather that you are likely to experience within several distinct areas are given on pages 213–232. These regions are:

1 South-West England and the Channel Islands
2 South-East England and East Anglia
3 The Midlands
4 North-West England and the Isle of Man
5 North-East England and Yorkshire
6 Wales
7 Ireland
8 Scotland

Using this book

In the pages that follow, a detailed assessment of the weather through the year is given. This is guided by the extremes of temperature and pressure that have been recorded in the past, as well as the weather that the UK saw during 2023. As well as this there are tables of times for sunrise, sunset, moonrise and moonset and diagrams showing twilight and Moon phases. Finally there is a list of weather-related anniversaries to watch out for each month. At the back of the book you can find more information about the climate in different parts of the British Isles, cloud types and measuring the weather, as well as a list of further reading.

Sunrise/Sunset & Moonrise/Moonset

For four dates within each month, tables show the times at
which the Sun and Moon rise and set at the four capital cities
in the United Kingdom: Belfast, Cardiff, Edinburgh and
London. For Edinburgh and London, the locations of specific
observatories are used, but not for Belfast and Cardiff, where
more general locations are employed. Interestingly, these
times are calculated taking into account the effect of refraction,
whereby light bends as it enters the atmosphere at a shallow
angle. This makes bodies like the Sun and Moon visible for a
few minutes before they have actually risen above the horizon,
and for a few minutes after they sink below it. However,
calculation of rising and setting times is complicated and
strongly depends on the precise location and altitude of the
observer, as well as atmospheric conditions, the height of any
landforms above the horizon, and other factors. Nevertheless,
the times shown will give a useful indication for most
purposes. Note that all the times in this book are calculated
astronomically, using what is known as Universal Time (UT),
sometimes known as Coordinated Universal Time (UTC). This
is identical to Greenwich Mean Time (GMT). The times given
do not take account of British Summer Time (BST).

The times given for the Moon may appear in either order,
depending on whether the Moon rises in the morning and sets
in the evening, or sets in the morning and rises again in the
evening. Note that which way round this is corresponds to the
Moon's phase; the New Moon by definition passes the meridian
around midday, and the Full Moon passes the meridian around
midnight. The time the Moon spends above the horizon also
varies in line with its phase each month, although the direction
of this correlation reverses through the year as the direction
of the Earth's tilt changes relative to the Sun (whose position
relative to the Moon dictates its phase). On rare occasions, there
is no time given for one or other event on a particular day.
This is because there can be over 24 hours between successive
moonrises or moonsets. The time is therefore shown as '–' and
a second line shows the time and azimuth at which the Moon
rose the day before, or the time and azimuth at which it
will set the following day.

Some effects are quite large. For example, at the summer solstice in 2025, sunrise is some 48 minutes later at Edinburgh than it is at Lerwick in the Shetlands. Sunset is some 32 minutes earlier on the same date.

Edinburgh & Lerwick: Comparison of sunrise & sunset times
A comparison of the timings of sunrise and sunset at Lerwick (latitude 60.16 N) and Edinburgh (latitude 55.9 N) in the following table gives an idea of how the times change with latitude. The timings are those at the equinoxes (20 March and 22 September in 2025) and the solstices (21 June and 21 December in 2025).

Location	Date	Rise	Azimuth	Set	Azimuth
Edinburgh	20 Mar 2025 (Thu)	06:14	89	18:26	272
Lerwick	20 Mar 2025 (Thu)	06:05	89	18:19	272
Edinburgh	21 Jun 2025 (Fri)	03:26	43	21:02	317
Lerwick	21 Jun 2025 (Fri)	02:38	34	21:34	326
Edinburgh	22 Sep 2025 (Mon)	05:58	89	18:11	271
Lerwick	22 Sep 2025 (Mon)	05:49	88	18:03	271
Edinburgh	21 Dec 2025 (Sun)	08:42	134	15:39	226
Lerwick	21 Dec 2025 (Sun)	09:08	141	14:57	219

Apart from the times, this table (and the monthly tables) also shows the azimuth of each event, which is an astronomical term indicating where the body concerned rises or sets. Azimuth is measured in degrees from north, through east, south and west, and then back to north, and the table below shows the azimuths for various compass points in the eastern and western sectors of the horizon. It is notable, of course, that although the times are different, the azimuth of sunrise is identical at both equinoxes, because the Sun is then crossing the celestial equator. At the solstices, both times and azimuths are different between the two locations.

The summer solstice at Quendale Bay in Shetland.

Table of azimuths

Degrees	Compass point		
Eastern horizon		*Western horizon*	
0°	N	180°	S
22° 30'	NNE	202° 30'	SSW
45°	NE	225°	SW
67° 30'	ENE	247° 30'	WSW
90°	E	270°	W
112° 30'	ESE	292° 30'	WNW
135°	SE	315°	NW
157° 30'	SSE	337° 30'	NNW

The actual latitude and longitude used in the calculations are shown in the following table. It will be seen that the altitudes of the observatories in Edinburgh (Royal Observatory Edinburgh, ROE) and London (Mill Hill Observatory) are quite considerable (that for ROE is particularly large) and these altitudes will affect the rising and setting times, which are calculated to apply to observers closer to sea level. (Generally, close to the observatories, such rising times will be slightly later, and setting times slightly earlier than those shown.)

Latitude and longitude of UK capital cities

City	Longitude	Latitude	Altitude
Belfast	5°56'00.0" W	54°36'00.0" N	3 m
Cardiff	3°11'00.0" W	51°30'00.0" N	3 m
Edinburgh (ROE)	3°11'00.0" W	55°55'30.0" N	146 m
London (Mill Hill)	0°14'24.0" W	51°36'48.0" N	81 m

Twilight and Moon phases

Besides the times of sunrise and sunset, twilight also varies
considerably from place to place, so the monthly diagrams
here show the duration of twilight at those four cities. During
the summer, twilight may persist throughout the night. This
applies everywhere in the United Kingdom, so two additional
yearly twilight diagrams are included (on pages 259 and 261):
one for Lerwick in the Shetlands and one for St Mary's in the
Scilly Isles. Although the hours of complete darkness increase
as one moves towards the equator, it will be seen that there is
full darkness nowhere in the British Isles at midsummer.

There are three recognised stages of twilight: *civil twilight*,
when the centre of the Sun is less than 6° below the horizon;
nautical twilight, when the Sun is between 6° and 12° below the
horizon; and *astronomical twilight*, when the Sun is between 12°
and 18° below the horizon. Full darkness occurs only when the
Sun is more than 18° below the horizon. The time at which civil
twilight begins is sometimes known in the UK as 'lighting-up
time'. Stars are generally invisible during civil twilight. During
nautical twilight, the very brightest stars are visible, but the
horizon is still visible; this allowed sailors to navigate, hence the
name for this stage. During astronomical twilight, the faintest
stars visible to the naked eye may be seen directly overhead,
but are lost at lower altitudes. They become visible only once
it is fully dark. The diagrams show the duration of twilight at
the various cities. Of the locations shown, during the summer
months there is astronomical twilight at most of the locations,
except at Lerwick, but there is never full darkness during the
summer anywhere in the British Isles. Twilight diagrams for
each of the four capital cities are shown every month, and full
yearly diagrams are shown on pages 259–261.

Also shown each month is the phase of the Moon for every
day, together with the age of the Moon, which is counted from
New Moon. For Full, New and Half Moons the exact time when
the phase occurs is given, and the timing of the New and Full
Moon is shown on the twilight diagrams as well (black and
white symbols, respectively). As may be seen, at most locations,
roughly half of New and Full Moon phases over the year may

come during daylight. For this reason, the exact phase may be invisible at that location. Additionally, some phases may occur while the Moon is below the horizon. This can be checked by referring to the table of Moonrise and Moonset times for each month.

The seasons

By convention, the year has always been divided into four seasons: spring, summer, autumn and winter. In the late eighteenth century, an early German meteorological society, the Societas Meteorologica Palatina, active in the Rhineland, defined the seasons as each consisting of three whole months, beginning before the equinoxes and solstices. So spring consisted of the months of March, April and May; summer of June, July and August; autumn of September, October and November; and winter of December, January and February. There has been a tendency by meteorologists to follow this convention to this day, with winter regarded as the three calendar months with the lowest temperatures in the northern hemisphere (December, January and February) and summer those with the warmest (June, July and August). Astronomers also generally regard the seasons as lasting three months, but centred on the dates of the equinoxes and solstices (20 March, 22 September and 21 June, 21 December in 2025).

Some ecologists tend to regard the year as divided into six seasons. Analysis of the prevailing weather types in Britain, however, suggests that there are five distinct seasons. Although the conditions associated with each season can in no way be specified as starting and ending on specific calendar dates, it is useful to give approximate dates. So in Britain, we have:

Early winter	20 November to 19 January
Late winter and early spring	20 January to 31 March
Spring and early summer	1 April to 17 June
High summer	18 June to 9 September
Autumn	10 September to 19 November

The weather and climatic systems characteristic of each
is described in the month in which the season begins. In
general, however, this division of the year gives an early winter
dominated by cool dry weather punctuated by the first storms
of the season; late winter containing the coldest days of the
year and the last of the wet westerlies; spring and early summer
bringing very changeable weather; high summer bringing hot
and settled conditions; and autumn marking the transition
back towards wet and windy weather.

On the following two pages can be found a summary of
the weather in 2023. More detailed data and descriptions are
given across the monthly chapters. This year, we have decided
to present the most recent full calendar year for which data is
available (2023), rather than simply the most recent instance
of each month as the book goes to print. This means there is
some overlap with the previous edition of the Weather Almanac,
but we hope that the result is a more logical picture of a year's
weather in Britain and Ireland.

The Weather in 2023

The year 2023 was described as 'very warm and rather wet' by the Met Office. The coldest weather occurred in mid-January and early March, and this was followed by a warm early summer, including record-breaking temperatures in June. Although July was less warm and quite wet, and August even saw two named storms, another extraordinary heatwave in early September meant the year was the second warmest on record for the UK, with only 2022 having been hotter. The minimum temperature was the highest on record, the annual mean temperature of 9.97°C was 0.83°C above the long-term average (based on temperatures from 1991 to 2020), and eight of the 12 months in the year were above average temperature. Temperature anomalies were highest in the west of the country, and for Wales and Northern Ireland this was the outright hottest year on record.

The autumn and early winter were wet and stormy, and contained the most impactful weather by far, as well as being the warmest of the year compared to historical trends. As well as the two named storms in August, there were a further six across October, November and December. The worst of these was Storm Babet in late October, which caused widespread severe flooding across eastern and central Scotland. Storm Ciarán in early November could have been even worse, but largely missed the UK to the south; western Europe was not so lucky, and saw a high death toll. The total rainfall for the year was 111 per cent of the average, making 2023 the eleventh wettest year since 1836. Only north-western Scotland was drier than normal.

The warm and unsettled weather in the second half of the year can be partly attributed to the ongoing El Niño event, which sees weaker winds in the eastern Pacific, resulting in warm water staying closer to the ocean surface for longer. This means more heat is transferred to the atmosphere, and the warmer and wetter air impacts weather around the globe.

However, the strength of this effect has almost certainly been exacerbated by human-induced climate change. The most recent findings from the Coupled Model Intercomparison Project found that the estimated frequency of the UK annual average temperature exceeding 9.97°C is approximately once in 460 years without human interference, but accounting for emissions-driven changes in the atmosphere this falls to once every three years. Our activity has therefore made a year like the one we've just had 150 times more likely. With the 1.5°C warming threshold compared to pre-industrial temperatures close to being breached, alarm bells are ringing.

Lowest temperature
-16°C
9 Mar 2023

Altnaharra

Depth snow lying
34 cm
18 & 19 Jan 2023

Loch Glascarnoch

Maximum 24-hr rainfall
129.5 mm
19 Oct 2023

Fettercairn

Highest temperature
33.5°C
10 Sep 2023

Faversham

Wind Gust
96 mph, 83 knots,
12 Apr 2023

Needles Old Battery

January

Introduction

As the New Year is born, the weather typically turns colder, with periods of extensive snow becoming more likely. In fact, the coldest and frostiest January on record was in 1963, with blizzards, snow drifts and temperatures plummeting as low as -19.4°C in Scotland. This winter was dubbed 'The Big Freeze of 1963' and even saw seawater freezing up to 6 kilometres away from the shore. The frigid weather persisted until early March, when mild air from the south-west finally brought a thaw to the country.

In typical years, snow is less widespread, thanks to the relatively warm water surrounding Britain and Ireland keeping our temperatures from falling too low. It goes without saying that cold air is a key ingredient for snow. As temperatures usually fall with rising altitude in the lowest level of the atmosphere, the tops of hills or mountains will often receive a dusting, while rain falls over the lower ground. For more widespread snow, Arctic maritime or polar continental air blowing in from the heart of Siberia is required. Occasionally, a persistent anticyclone and clear skies may also allow temperatures to fall low enough for snow.

The second ingredient is moisture. This can be picked up as air travels over the relatively warm North Sea, resulting in snow showers, especially as they move inland and hit cold air. Otherwise, the cold air must meet frontal rain for snow to fall. This often occurs when mild, moist air from the south-west collides with cold air already in place. Rain along the frontal boundary will turn to snow as it hits the cold air, and this can be very difficult for forecasters to predict.

To meteorologists and astrologists, this month falls in the middle of winter. However, in 1950, climatologist Professor Hubert Lamb published a scientific paper suggesting that prevailing weather types in the British Isles can be categorised into five natural seasons. He analysed more than 18,000 daily weather charts looking for patterns and trends that appeared each year. By this system, 'late winter and early spring' begins around 20 January and continues until the end of March. It typically brings a mixture of unsettled, stormy periods punctuated by spells of settled weather, which can be very cold, depending on where the air is coming from. Occurrences of westerly dominated conditions tend to tail off through this season as cold northerly or easterly winds become more prevalent.

In Europe, the Full Moon in January is generally known as the 'Wolf Moon', named after the howls of wolves searching for food in mid-winter. This tradition of naming moons originates from various indigenous and cultural practices, and often reflects the ongoing seasonal changes. Although wolves were hunted to extinction in Britain at some point in the eighteenth century, their presence here and in Ireland is still remembered by the naming of January's Full Moon.

Lapse rate
The change in a property with increasing altitude. In meteorology, this is usually the change in temperature. In the troposphere (the lowest layer of the atmosphere), this is a decrease in temperature with an increase in height. This is defined as a positive lapse rate. In the stratosphere (the next higher layer) there is an overall increase in temperature with height, giving a negative lapse rate.

Weather Extremes in January

Country	Temp.	Location	Date
Maximum temperature			
England	17.6°C	Eynsford (Kent)	27 Jan 2003
Wales	18.3°C	Aber (Gwynedd)	10 Jan 1971 27 Jan 1958
Scotland	18.3°C	Aboyne (Aberdeenshire) Inchmarlo (Kincardineshire)	26 Jan 2003
Northern Ireland	16.4°C	Knockarevan (County Fermanagh)	26 Jan 2003
Minimum temperature			
England	-26.1°C	Newport (Shropshire)	10 Jan 1982
Wales	-23.3°C	Rhayader (Powys)	21 Jan 1940
Scotland	-27.2°C	Braemar (Aberdeenshire)	10 Jan 1982
Northern Ireand	-17.5°C	Magherally (County Down)	1 Jan 1979

Country	Pressure	Location	Date
Maximum pressure			
Scotland	1053.6 hPa	Aberdeen Observatory	31 Jan 1902
Minimum pressure			
Scotland	925.6 hPa	Ochtertyre (Perthshire)	26 Jan 1884

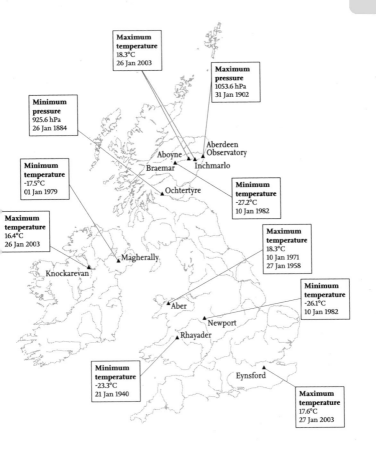

Maximum
temperature
18.3°C
26 Jan 2003

Maximum
pressure
1053.6 hPa
31 Jan 1902

Minimum
pressure
925.6 hPa
26 Jan 1884

Minimum
temperature
-17.5°C
01 Jan 1979

Maximum
temperature
16.4°C
26 Jan 2003

Aberdeen
Observatory
Aboyne
Braemar   Inchmarlo

Ochtertyre

Minimum
temperature
-27.2°C
10 Jan 1982

Maximum
temperature
18.3°C
10 Jan 1971
27 Jan 1958

Knockarevan

Magherally

Minimum
temperature
-26.1°C
10 Jan 1982

Aber
Newport

Rhayader

Minimum
temperature
-23.3°C
21 Jan 1940

Eynsford

Maximum
temperature
17.6°C
27 Jan 2003

The Weather in January 2023

Observation	Location	Date
Max. temperature 15.8°C	Dyce (Aberdeenshire)	24 January
Min. temperature -10.4°C	Drumnadrochit (Inverness-shire)	19 January
Most rainfall 100.2 mm	Maerdy Water Works (Mid Glamorgan)	11 January
Highest gust 83 mph (134 kph/72 kt)	Needles Old Battery (Isle of Wight)	12 January
Greatest snow depth 34 cm	Loch Glascarnoch (Ross & Cromarty)	18 and 19 January

January was a month of two halves. The beginning of the month continued with the mild, unsettled weather that had ended December 2022. This was caused by a series of deep depressions interrupted by ridges of high pressure over the Atlantic, while the jet stream was weaker than usual and located towards Europe. The highest minimum temperature occurred on the 5th, with St Mary's Airport on the Isles of Scilly recording a minimum of 11.7°C.

With this came heavy rain, especially from the 10th to 13th. Some places received their average monthly rainfall for January within the first two weeks. Impacts on travel included road closures and flooded rail lines in South Wales and the Midlands and Somerset Levels also experienced flooding. Maerdy Water Treatment Works in Mid Glamorgan received over 100 millimetres of rainfall on the 11th. Wind speeds were also high during this period, with northern Scotland seeing gusts over 50 mph (80.5 kph/43.4 knots) across wide areas.

The second half of the month saw temperatures fall and rainfall decrease sharply as winds turned northerly. Parts of Scotland recorded significant snowfall (34 centimetres fell at

Loch Glascarnoch on the 18th and 19th), as did Cornwall and North Wales when heavy snow showers arrived from the Irish Sea.

Once the worst of the cold snap passed, the weather for the end of the month was more benign. By the 23rd, high pressure had established itself over the south of the UK, with colder weather persisting and several fog warnings issued. High volumes of surface water remained from earlier in the month in some places. In the north of England and Scotland the highest maxima of the month were witnessed (15.8°C at Dyce, Aberdeenshire, on the 24th), and the milder weather saw some rain return.

Overall, despite these swinging extremes, mean temperatures were close to average. The overall mean was 0.4°C above the 1991–2020 average, with northern parts of England and Wales the most so, but nowhere saw anomalies of greater than 1°C. Rainfall was also close to average, but this doesn't tell the whole story; parts of western England and Wales received 150 per cent of their normal monthly rainfall, while eastern Scotland and north-east England received only 50 per cent. England saw its second sunniest January on record, and the UK as a whole saw 133 per cent of its average sun for the month.

Nacreous clouds
Brilliantly coloured clouds (also known as 'mother-of-pearl' clouds) that are occasionally seen at sunset or sunrise. They occur in the lowest region of the stratosphere at altitudes of 15–30 kilometres. They arise when wave motion at altitude causes water vapour to freeze onto suitable nuclei at very low temperatures (below -83°C).

Sunrise and Sunset 2025

Location	Date	Rise	Azimuth °	Set	Azimuth °
Belfast					
	1 Jan (Wed)	08:46	131	16:08	229
	11 Jan (Sat)	08:40	128	16:23	232
	21 Jan (Tue)	08:29	124	16:40	236
	31 Jan (Fri)	08:14	119	17:00	241
Cardiff					
	1 Jan (Wed)	08:18	127	16:14	233
	11 Jan (Sat)	08:14	125	16:27	235
	21 Jan (Tue)	08:05	122	16:43	238
	31 Jan (Fri)	07:52	117	17:00	243
Edinburgh					
	1 Jan (Wed)	08:43	132	15:49	228
	11 Jan (Sat)	08:37	130	16:04	230
	21 Jan (Tue)	08:25	126	16:23	234
	31 Jan (Fri)	08:08	121	16:44	240
London					
	1 Jan (Wed)	08:06	127	16:02	233
	11 Jan (Sat)	08:02	125	16:15	235
	21 Jan (Tue)	07:53	122	16:30	238
	31 Jan (Fri)	07:39	117	16:48	243

Note that all times are in Universal Time (UT), otherwise known as Greenwich Mean Time (GMT). These times do not take Summer Time (BST) into account.

Moonrise and Moonset 2025

Location	Date	Rise	Azimuth °	Set	Azimuth °
Belfast					
	1 Jan (Wed)	10:30	136	17:34	227
	11 Jan (Sat)	13:05	36	07:13	233
	21 Jan (Tue)	00:42	109	10:42	247
	31 Jan (Fri)	09:19	109	19:48	256
Cardiff					
	1 Jan (Wed)	09:59	132	17:42	230
	11 Jan (Sat)	13:20	41	06:35	318
	21 Jan (Tue)	00:23	107	10:39	249
	31 Jan (Fri)	09:01	108	19:49	257
Edinburgh					
	1 Jan (Wed)	10:30	138	17:13	224
	11 Jan (Sat)	12:39	33	07:15	326
	21 Jan (Tue)	00:33	109	10:27	247
	31 Jan (Fri)	09:12	110	19:33	255
London					
	1 Jan (Wed)	09:47	132	17:29	230
	11 Jan (Sat)	13:07	41	06:22	318
	21 Jan (Tue)	00:10	107	10:27	249
	31 Jan (Fri)	08:49	108	19:29	256

Note that all times are in Universal Time (UT), otherwise known as Greenwich Mean Time (GMT). These times do not take Summer Time (BST) into account.

Twilight Diagrams 2025

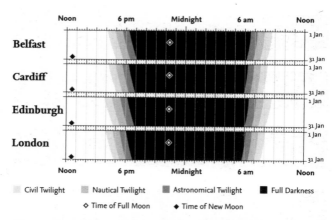

| Noon | 6 pm | Midnight | 6 am | Noon |

Belfast

Cardiff

Edinburgh

London

| | Civil Twilight | | Nautical Twilight | | Astronomical Twilight | ■ Full Darkness |

◇ Time of Full Moon   ◆ Time of New Moon

The exact times of the Moon's major phases are shown on the diagrams opposite.

Polar cell

One of the two cells, farthest from the equator, where cold air spreads out from the poles, heading in the general direction of the equator. The winds are easterly. This air meets the air in the Ferrel cells at the polar fronts, which tend to vary in latitude, and which are where the all-important depressions form.

The Moon's Phases and Ages 2025

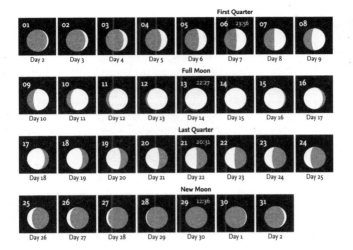

First Quarter

01	02	03	04	05	06 23:56	07	08
Day 2	Day 3	Day 4	Day 5	Day 6	Day 7	Day 8	Day 9

Full Moon

09	10	11	12	13 22:27	14	15	16
Day 10	Day 11	Day 12	Day 13	Day 14	Day 15	Day 16	Day 17

Last Quarter

17	18	19	20	21 20:31	22	23	24
Day 18	Day 19	Day 20	Day 21	Day 22	Day 23	Day 24	Day 25

New Moon

25	26	27	28	29 12:36	30	31
Day 26	Day 27	Day 28	Day 29	Day 30	Day 1	Day 2

Polar front
The area where cold air from the poles meets warmer air that has
spread out from the sub-tropical high-pressure regions. The conflict
between the two types of air creates depressions which bring most
of the changeable weather to countries in the middle latitudes.

January – In This Month

1 January 1611 – Johannes Kepler published his treatise *The Six-Cornered Snowflake* as a New Year gift to the Holy Roman Emperor Rudolf II.

2 January 1928 – The *Aberdeen Press and Journal* reported on the 'Great Snow-up' in Kent, with workers pictured digging through head-high banks of snow to reach a village that had been cut off since Christmas.

2 January 1976 – A gale caused severe wind damage and coastal flooding across western Europe. Among the damage in the UK were a light aircraft blown onto the adjacent railway at Southend Airport, a pinnacle from the tower of Worcester Cathedral crashing through the transept roof and scaffolding surrounding London's Old Vic theatre being torn down.

10 January 1344 – William Merle wrote the last entry in his weather journal, the first daily meteorological record in existence.

16 January 1917 – Newquay saw 13 centimetres of snow in what was a very cold January, especially in Wales and the north-west of England. The River Mersey partly froze.

17–20 January 1881 – A severe blizzard struck southern England. Newport on the Isle of Wight saw 86 centimetres of snow, and there were reports of drifts over 3 metres deep at Cowes. Buildings collapsed under the weight of the snow and hundreds of kilometres of railway were closed.

23 January 1909 – Snow blocked the West Highland rail line, with one train stuck for a day and a half. The passengers were without food, and passed the time playing bagpipes.

26 January 1939 – Ipswich received 24 hours of continuous rainfall, resulting in catastrophic flooding. Three people died and thousands of homes were inundated with up to 1.5 metres of water.

29 January 1817 – William Ferrel was born, who correlated the motion of the Earth with that of the atmosphere, and after whom the Ferrel Cell is named.

Benjamin Franklin

A Founding Father of the United States, many remember Benjamin Franklin for his development of the US constitution and government, including drafting and signing the Declaration of Independence. There is no doubt that he was one of the most influential people in American history. However, his contributions to the field of science and meteorology go largely unsung.

Born on 17 January 1706 in Boston, Benjamin Franklin only attended school until he was ten. He then worked in his father's candle and soap shop for two years, before taking on an apprenticeship in his older brother's printing shop. It was here that he wrote the letters published under his first pseudonym, Ms Silence Dogood. Over the following years, Franklin continued to work in printing, spending time in New York, London and Philadelphia, the latter becoming the city in which he would spend most of his life. At 26 years old, he published his first Almanac, 'Poor Richard's Almanack', under the pseudonym Richard Saunders. It contained the usual weather forecasts, astronomical information and calendar, while also including recipes, advice and jokes. It became a best-seller, and Franklin published further editions for the next 25 years.

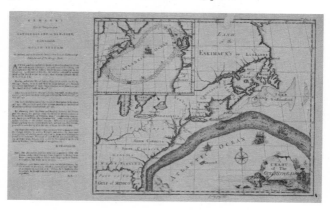

Map of the Gulf Stream by Benjamin Franklin.

In 1753, after 15 years' service as Postmaster of Philadelphia, Franklin was appointed Deputy Postmaster for the American Colonies. It was this, perhaps, which led him to his later discovery and naming of the Gulf Stream.

The Gulf Stream is a fast-flowing Atlantic Ocean current that originates from the Gulf of Mexico, transporting warm waters through the Straits of Florida and up the eastern coast of the United States. It is often credited for the mild waters surrounding Britain and Ireland. However, it is more accurate to attribute these to the North Atlantic Current, or Drift, which is the eastward extension of the Gulf Stream.

Benjamin Franklin Drawing Electricity from the Sky *by Benjamin West.*

As Franklin made frequent journeys across the Atlantic Ocean during his time as Postmaster, he was given ample opportunity to observe the current first hand. Noting that his westbound trips took around two weeks longer than his journeys east, and that British postal boats often took longer to reach the United States than American merchant ships, he put the question to his cousin, Timothy Folger. Folger, who had also spent plenty of time at sea, captaining both merchant and whaling ships, had observed the current and gave his cousin directions on how to avoid it. Franklin subsequently charted and published information about the Gulf Stream, sharing it with the British Royal Mail Ships, whose captains largely ignored the advice.

Aside from the Gulf Stream, Franklin also had a keen interest in meteorology; in particular, lightning. His experiment of flying a kite in a thunderstorm led him to invent the lightning rod. He also made observations on weather patterns and the aurora borealis.

February

Introduction

As the last month of meteorological winter, February typically continues on a cold vein. Braemar, a village nestled in the heart of the Cairngorms in Scotland, has fallen to -27.2°C twice since records began: once in January, and once on 11 February 1895, which was, incidentally, the coldest February on record and considered by some climatologists to be the end of the 'Little Ice Age'. Although not technically an ice age, it was a time where temperatures in northern Europe cooled, leading to a series of harsh winters in Britain and Ireland.

Although there have been some cold winters since, human-induced climate change, kickstarted by the Industrial Revolution, means average temperatures are on the up. Naturally, this is accompanied by the breaking of temperature records, as was seen in February 2019, which saw the warmest winter day on record as temperatures topped 20°C for the first time ever in February. Three sites broke this record, the warmest of which was Porthmadog in Gwynedd, west Wales, reaching 20.8°C. This was thanks to a large blocking high sitting over north-western Europe, combined with a deep trough over the Atlantic. The resultant south to south-westerly air flow brought mild air all the way up to the UK from north-west Africa.

While high pressure brought clear skies and sunshine during the lengthening days, it also led to some extraordinary diurnal temperature ranges – the difference between the daytime high and night-time low. The air was very dry and under clear skies, overnight temperatures plummeted to -2.3°C in Bala, Wales. As the Sun rose, the mercury rose with it, and by the afternoon, temperatures had climbed to 20°C, bringing a diurnal temperature range of more than 22°C. This is typical of late winter and early spring, where days are becoming warmer, but nights are still long enough to bring significant cooling.

As warmth builds, February also sees the return of land-based convection – whereby heat from the Sun warms air close to the ground, causing it to rise. As it rises, the air condenses, forming cumulus clouds and often showers. From around mid-month, or Valentine's Day, sufficient heating can see showers bubbling up across southern Britain. This season of surface-based convection generally continues all the way through until mid-October before tailing off, as days shorten and the heat reaching us from the Sun is no longer strong enough to trigger the effect.

Despite this, February is typically the driest of winter months, although as anyone who has lived in the UK will know, the weather can still be incredibly variable. Depending on the strength and position of the jet stream, Atlantic depressions may still barrel into Britain and Ireland through February. Often, when conditions are right, storms may develop in quick succession, as seen in February 2020, when Storm Dennis followed in hot pursuit of Storm Ciara. Both storms brought widespread flooding, and even after Dennis cleared, the weather remained wet and windy, resulting in the wettest February on record.

F

Anemometer
Any device that measures wind speeds, generally in a horizontal direction. There are various types. The form most commonly seen is probably the type that has three rotating cups. Other versions use propellors, differences in pressure or the transmission of sound or heat. Certain devices (particularly sonic anemometers) are able to measure the vertical motion of the air, as well as motion in a horizontal direction.

Weather Extremes in February

Country	Temp.	Location	Date
Maximum temperature			
England	21.2°C	Kew Gardens (London)	26 Feb 2019
Wales	20.8°C	Porthmadog (Gwynedd)	26 Feb 2019
Scotland	18.3°C	Aboyne (Aberdeenshire)	21 Feb 2019
Northern Ireland	17.8°C	Bryansford (County Down)	13 Feb 1998
Minimum temperature			
England	-22.2°C	Scaleby (Cumbria) Ketton (East Midlands)	19 Feb 1892 8 Feb 1895
Wales	-20.0°C	Welshpool (Powys)	2 Feb 1954
Scotland	-27.2°C	Braemar (Aberdeenshire)	11 Feb 1895
Northern Ireland	-15.6°C	Garvagh, Moneydig (County Londonderry)	20 Feb 1955

Country	Pressure	Location	Date
Maximum pressure			
Scotland	1052.9 hPa	Aberdeen Observatory	1 Feb 1902
Minimum pressure			
Republic of Ireland	942.3 hPa	Midleton (County Cork)	4 Feb 1951

F

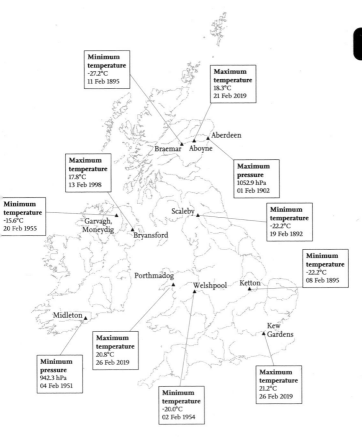

Minimum temperature
-27.2°C
11 Feb 1895

Maximum temperature
18.3°C
21 Feb 2019

Aberdeen

Braemar Aboyne

Maximum pressure
1052.9 hPa
01 Feb 1902

Maximum temperature
17.8°C
13 Feb 1998

Minimum temperature
-15.6°C
20 Feb 1955

Garvagh, Moneydig

Scaleby

Minimum temperature
-22.2°C
19 Feb 1892

Bryansford

Minimum temperature
-22.2°C
08 Feb 1895

Porthmadog

Welshpool Ketton

Midleton

Kew Gardens

Minimum pressure
942.3 hPa
04 Feb 1951

Maximum temperature
20.8°C
26 Feb 2019

Maximum temperature
21.2°C
26 Feb 2019

Minimum temperature
-20.0°C
02 Feb 1954

The Weather in February 2023

Observation	Location	Date
Max. temperature 17.2°C	Pershore (Hereford & Worcester)	17 February
Min. temperature -8.5°C	Tulloch Bridge (Inverness-shire)	27 February
Most rainfall 45.6 mm	Cassley (Sutherland)	2 February
Highest gust 83 mph (134 kph/72 kt)	Baltasound No.2 (Shetland)	3 February
Greatest snow depth 1 cm	Fettercairn, Glensaugh No. 2 (Kincardineshire) and Oyne No. 2 (Aberdeenshire)	18 February

The start of the month saw strong westerly winds, with heavy rain disrupting train and ferry services in western Scotland. Cassley in Sutherland saw 45.6 millimetres of rain on the 2nd. Thereafter, February was remarkably dry, being dominated by a period of high pressure and predominantly anticyclonic. A cold easterly allowed temperatures to fall dramatically in the south, with South Newington in Oxfordshire recording a minimum of -8.4°C.

The middle of the month saw a series of depressions crossing the UK, bringing some rain along with very mild air.

All four nations saw maxima in the mid-teens. The arrival of Storm Otto (named by the Danish weather service) on the 17th brought strong winds, with gusts exceeding 60 mph (97 kph/84 knots) in many places across northern and eastern Scotland, north-east England and Yorkshire. Inverbervie in Kincardineshire saw gusts of 83 mph (134 kph/116 knots), and power outages affected as many as 60,000 homes according to some estimates. Over 1,000 were still without power the following morning. East Coast Main Line rail services were also severely disrupted by damage to overhead wires, and rural road networks impacted by fallen trees. Even major road routes were disrupted, with several bridges in Scotland imposing height limits, and numerous lorries reportedly overturning on the A1(M).

Later in the month the high pressure zone was re-established, although winds were more northerly bringing temperatures down and widespread night-time frosts. No further adverse impacts were recorded, with the most notable phenomenon later in the month being an unusually prominent auroral display visible across much of Britain on the 26th.

Overall, dryness and mildness characterised the month. Central and southern England saw only 20 per cent of their average rainfall for February. Although rainfall was closer to normal further north and west, the UK as a whole received an average of only 43.4 millimetres of rain over the month, just 45 per cent of the February mean. Only north-west Scotland received more rain than average, and for the UK it was the driest February for 30 years. There was almost no snow, with the greatest depth recorded being 1 centimetre at Fettercairn on the 18th. Temperatures were well above average, with the provisional UK mean of 5.8°C some 1.7°C above the 1991–2020 average. This anomaly was particularly pronounced in Scotland and Northern Ireland, with mean minimums as high as 2.3°C above the 1991–2020 average.

Sunrise and Sunset 2025

Location	Date	Rise	Azimuth °	Set	Azimuth °
Belfast					
	1 Feb (Sat)	08:12	119	17:02	241
	11 Feb (Tue)	07:53	113	17:23	247
	21 Feb (Fri)	07:31	107	17:44	253
	28 Feb (Fri)	07:14	102	17:58	258
Cardiff					
	1 Feb (Sat)	07:50	117	17:02	243
	11 Feb (Tue)	07:33	112	17:20	249
	21 Feb (Fri)	07:14	106	17:39	254
	28 Feb (Fri)	06:59	102	17:51	259
Edinburgh					
	1 Feb (Sat)	08:06	120	16:46	240
	11 Feb (Tue)	07:46	114	17:08	246
	21 Feb (Fri)	07:23	108	17:30	253
	28 Feb (Fri)	07:06	103	17:45	257
London					
	1 Feb (Sat)	07:38	117	16:50	243
	11 Feb (Tue)	07:21	112	17:08	249
	21 Feb (Fri)	07:02	106	17:26	254
	28 Feb (Fri)	06:47	102	17:39	259

Note that all times are in Universal Time (UT), otherwise known as Greenwich Mean Time (GMT). These times do not take Summer Time (BST) into account.

Moonrise and Moonset 2025

Location	Date	Rise	Azimuth °	Set	Azimuth °
Belfast					
	1 Feb (Sat)	09:28	98	21:19	268
	11 Feb (Tue)	15:52	53	08:01	310
	21 Feb (Fri)	03:35	140	09:45	218
	28 Feb (Fri)	07:36	103	18:50	262
Cardiff					
	1 Feb (Sat)	09:14	97	21:08	268
	11 Feb (Tue)	15:56	56	07:33	307
	21 Feb (Fri)	02:59	136	09:59	232
	28 Feb (Fri)	07:20	102	18:41	263
Edinburgh					
	1 Feb (Sat)	09:18	98	21:07	268
	11 Feb (Tue)	15:33	51	07:58	312
	21 Feb (Fri)	03:36	143	09:21	216
	28 Feb (Fri)	07:27	104	18:37	262
London					
	1 Feb (Sat)	09:02	97	20:55	268
	11 Feb (Tue)	15:43	56	07:21	307
	21 Feb (Fri)	02:47	136	09:46	223
	28 Feb (Fri)	07:08	103	18:28	263

F

Note that all times are in Universal Time (UT), otherwise known as Greenwich Mean Time (GMT). These times do not take Summer Time (BST) into account.

Twilight Diagrams 2025

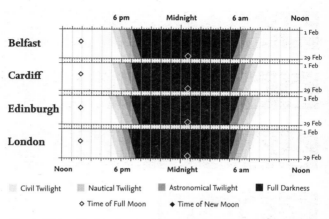

The exact times of the Moon's major phases are shown on the diagrams opposite.

Doldrums

The doldrums are a zone of reduced winds, generally located over the equatorial region, although moving north and south with the seasons. Air in the Doldrums is largely rising, because solar heating and horizontal motion across the surface is reduced or non-existent.

The Moon's Phases and Ages 2025

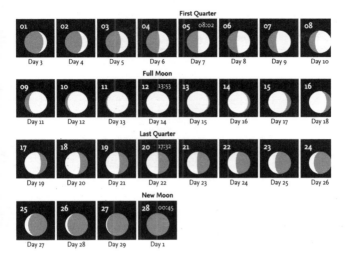

First Quarter

01	02	03	04	05 08:02	06	07	08
Day 3	Day 4	Day 5	Day 6	Day 7	Day 8	Day 9	Day 10

Full Moon

09	10	11	12 13:53	13	14	15	16
Day 11	Day 12	Day 13	Day 14	Day 15	Day 16	Day 17	Day 18

Last Quarter

17	18	19	20 17:32	21	22	23	24
Day 19	Day 20	Day 21	Day 22	Day 23	Day 24	Day 25	Day 26

New Moon

25	26	27	28 00:45
Day 27	Day 28	Day 29	Day 1

F

Cyclone
Technically, a name for any circulation of air around a low-pressure centre. (Depressions are also known as 'extratropical cyclones'.) The term is also used specifically for a tropical, revolving storm in the Indian Ocean, known as a 'hurricane' over the North Atlantic Ocean or eastern Pacific Ocean. The term 'typhoon' is used for systems in the western Pacific that affect northern Australia and Asia. The term 'tropical cyclones' applies to all such revolving systems.

February – In This Month

7 February 1483 – Yuriy Drohobych published his *Prognostic Assessment of the Year 1483*. Although astrological in nature, the work correctly predicted two lunar eclipses and observed that climatic conditions depend on latitude.

7 February 1795 – The 'great frost' that had lasted the previous month and a half came to an end. As the ice partly thawed it created what Thomas Barker, a contemporary diarist, described as 'a greater flood than any remembered, which did more damage to the bridges all over the kingdom than was ever known'. The flooding was also ruinous to winter crops, which had already been damaged by the severe frosts.

9 February 1855 – After a night of heavy snowfall, people in south Devon reported mysterious hoofprints in the snow. The tracks covered between 60 and 160 kilometres and traversed houses, rivers, haystacks and other obstacles without deviating. They were superstitiously dubbed the 'Devil's Footprints'.

11 February 1947 – The government discussed bringing in the army to use flamethrowers to clear packed snow and ice that was blocking roads and railways. Instead, gas turbines were fitted to the front of railway carriages to clear the way in a less destructive manner.

12 February 1850 – William Morris Davis, a geologist and meteorologist often called the 'father of American geography', was born. Although he made important observations about the cycle of erosion, his wider theories of geomorphology were later superseded, and he was discredited for his advancement of scientific racism.

16 February 1962 – The Great Sheffield Gale wrought havoc on the city, killing four people. The extratropical cyclone responsible went on to cause extensive flooding in Hamburg, where 315 people died and 60,000 homes were destroyed.

23 February 2017 – Storm Doris brought wind speeds above 90 mph (145 kph/78 knots) in England and Wales and heavy snowfall across Scotland.

24 February 1838 – A severe gale caused the Bude breakwater to give way. The breakwater had been constructed with too steep a slope, and the mortar had been weakened by frosts over the winter.

26 February 1884 – The 'Great English Earthquake' occurred in Colchester, Essex. The quake lasted for around 20 seconds and measured 4.6 on the Richter scale, with the effects felt across England, Belgium and northern France. Over 1,000 buildings were damaged, some as far away as Ipswich.

26–27 February 1903 – Storm Ulysses tore across the UK and Ireland. Examining historic records, scientists have estimated that it produced the strongest winds ever seen in the UK. The effects, which included large trees being blown over in Dublin, inspired a passage in James Joyce's novel *Ulysses*, hence the later nickname.

The Last Frost Fair

As our climate changes and winters become warmer and wetter, it is hard to imagine a time in which the winters were so cold that the River Thames froze over. And not just a thin layer of ice, but thick enough for a funfair to be held on the frozen river.

During the 'Little Ice Age', roughly between the early fourteenth century and mid-nineteenth century, the Thames was recorded to have frozen at least 24 times. However, historical accounts suggest that social gatherings were held on the river as early as 250 CE. The first official frost fair is said to have been held in 1608, as this is the first recorded use of the term 'frost fair'. At least five major frost fairs were held over the following 200 years, as well as reports of many smaller ones.

On 1 February 1814, although Londoners did not know it at the time, the last frost fair was held. Thousands of people turned up to witness this marvel and step onto the ice. There was dancing, ice skating and bowling. Tradespeople set up makeshift tents to sell their wares, offering gingerbread, roast

Gingerbread bought at the Last Frost Fair, 1814.

mutton (cooked on the ice!), toys and books, while temporary bars sold beer and gin. And perhaps, most incredible of all, several eyewitnesses reported seeing an elephant being walked across the frozen river near Blackfriars Bridge. Around a dozen printing presses were set up on the Thames and one entrepreneur, George Davis, sold copies of a commemorative book, *Frostiana*, while another printed the following poem:

You that walk here, and do design to tell
Your children's children what this year befell,
Come, buy this print, and it will then be seen
That such a year as this has seldom been.

And such a year never was again, for the ice began to break up during a rapid thaw on 5 February. Rain began to fall and the sound of ominous cracking was heard. The river claimed many of the booths that had been installed upon the ice and at least

The Fair on the Thames, Feb'y 4th 1814 *by Luke Clenell.*

two young men lost their lives. Although the Thames froze once more, six years later, no frost fair was held – maybe because the last one had come to such a tragic end.

Perhaps the river would have continued to freeze several more times, if it wasn't for the demolition of the Old London Bridge in 1825, and the subsequent construction of embankments through the remainder of the 1800s. The old bridge had many small arches, which slowed the flow of the river, making freezing easier. Nowadays, the river is narrower and deeper, with faster-flowing waters. This, combined with our warming climate, means we are unlikely to see scenes like this ever again.

March

Introduction

While days continue to lengthen and temperatures rise, March brings the beginning of meteorological spring. It is typically seen as a season of transition and gets its name from the flowers that 'spring up' at this time of year. The earliest use of the word has been dated back to the fourteenth century, where it was referred to as 'springing time', replacing the Old English description of the 'Lenten season', which refers to the lengthening daylight hours, and for which the Christian fast of 'Lent' is named.

The position of the jet stream dictates the weather during March. An active jet stream centred over Britain and Ireland will continue to bring low pressure systems in from the Atlantic. However, the frequency of depressions tracking across the country often tails off as March progresses. High pressure is likely to develop but it doesn't necessarily mean bright sunshine and fine weather. In winter and early spring, when the ground cools significantly overnight, low cloud and fog may form as the air above the ground cools and condenses. The warmth from the Sun at this time of year is not enough to 'burn off' the fog during the day, and this moisture can become trapped. When this occurs, temperatures close to the ground are colder, and increase with height – known as a temperature inversion. Beneath the inversion and without strong winds to disperse them, the dull conditions can persist for several days, a phenomenon known as 'anticyclonic gloom'. This causes quite a headache for weather forecasters, whose computer models struggle to predict what will happen to the cloud cover. In the renewable energy sector, it is referred to as 'dunkelflaute', which means 'dark doldrums' or 'dark wind lull', and is considered particularly frustrating, as neither solar nor wind are likely to generate much power.

While showers are likely to develop at times, lightning activity is typically low in March. This is because temperatures are not yet high enough to trigger the deep convection required for thunder and lightning. The popular weather lore, 'When March blows its horn, your barn will be filled with grain and corn', refers to thunderstorms developing, and links it to a fruitful harvest to come. However, although thunderstorms suggest that it is warmer than average for the time of year, this hasn't been linked to any longer-term weather trends.

M

The Full Moon in March (14 March in 2025) is known as a 'Worm Moon', the naming giving another nod to the end of winter, as the warming ground conditions encourage the appearance of worms in the soil. The Full Moon will also coincide with a partial lunar eclipse in 2025, while a partial solar eclipse will occur later in the month on 29 March.

Hurricane
The term used for a tropical cyclone in the North Atlantic Ocean or eastern Pacific Ocean. Hurricanes (indeed all tropical cyclones) are driven by high sea-surface temperatures, and cannot occur over the British Isles.

Weather Extremes in March

Country	Temp.	Location	Date
Maximum temperature			
England	25.6°C	Mepal (Cambridgeshire)	29 Mar 1968
Wales	23.9°C	Prestatyn (Denbighshire) Ceinws (Powys)	29 Mar 1965
Scotland	23.6°C	Aboyne (Aberdeenshire)	27 Mar 2012
Northern Ireland	21.8°C	Armagh (County Armagh)	29 Mar 1965
Minimum temperature			
England	-21.1°C	Houghall (County Durham)	4 Mar 1947
Wales	-21.7°C	Corwen (Denbighshire)	3 Mar 1965
Scotland	-22.8°C	Logie Coldstone (Aberdeenshire)	14 Mar 1958
Northern Ireland	-14.8°C	Katesbridge (County Down)	2 Mar 2001

Country	Pressure	Location	Date
Maximum pressure			
Republic of Ireland	1051.3 hPa	Malin Head (County Donegal)	29 Mar 2020
Minimum pressure			
Scotland	946.2 hPa	Wick (Caithness)	9 Mar 1876

M

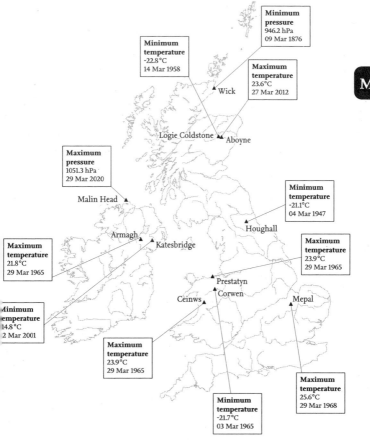

Minimum pressure
946.2 hPa
09 Mar 1876

Minimum temperature
-22.8°C
14 Mar 1958

Maximum temperature
23.6°C
27 Mar 2012

Wick

Logie Coldstone ▲ Aboyne

Maximum pressure
1051.3 hPa
29 Mar 2020

Malin Head ▲

Minimum temperature
-21.1°C
04 Mar 1947

Houghall ▲

Armagh ▲ Katesbridge

Maximum temperature
21.8°C
29 Mar 1965

Maximum temperature
23.9°C
29 Mar 1965

Minimum temperature
14.8°C
2 Mar 2001

Prestatyn
Corwen

Ceinws

Mepal

Maximum temperature
23.9°C
29 Mar 1965

Maximum temperature
25.6°C
29 Mar 1968

Minimum temperature
-21.7°C
03 Mar 1965

The Weather in March 2023

Observation	Location	Date
Max. temperature 17.8°C	Santon Downham (Suffolk)	30 March
Min. temperature -16.0°C	Altnaharra No 2 (Sutherland)	9 March
Most rainfall 118.6 mm	Honister Pass (Cumbria)	12 March
Most sunshine 11.9 hrs	Bishopton (Renfrewshire)	27 March
Highest gust 82 mph (132 kph/71 kt)	Capel Curig No. 3 (Conway)	21 March
Greatest snow depth 32 cm	Buxton, Derbyshire	10 March

With high pressure continuing, March began as February had ended: cold and dry. Some snow arrived on a surge of Arctic air on the 6th and 7th, and from the 8th onwards things became more unsettled as moist, milder air intruded from the south. The boundary between these two systems witnessed more snow, with disruption reported at Bristol airport and schools closed in large parts of Scotland. In Derbyshire a major incident was declared on the 9th, and mountain rescue teams were deployed to help motorists trapped between Buxton and Ashbourne. The 9th also saw the lowest minimum, as temperatures at Altnaharrra in Sutherland hit -16°C. The following morning saw 32 cm of snow lying at Buxton.

After persisting for several days, the cold northern air was finally displaced by the 16th as the high pressure drifted away towards Greenland. In its place a series of Atlantic depressions drove across the UK. The middle of the month was therefore milder though unsettled, with westerly and south-westerly winds and maximum temperatures exceeding 16°C in all four nations. Several bands of rain in quick succession saw volumes in excess of 50 mm at numerous sites on the 12th. Honister Pass in Cumbria (a notoriously wet site) received more than twice that, with 118.6 mm. More heavy rain on the 18th and high spring tides on the 22nd brought widespread flooding everywhere from South Yorkshire to Cornwall.

Thereafter followed a few days of finer weather, with 11.9 hours of sunshine recorded in Bishopton, Renfrewshire on the 27th, but the very end of the month became unsettled again. A low pressure zone passed close to the south of the UK, bringing strong winds. In Cornwall there were reports of power outages and trees blown down, but for most of the UK the end of the month was dull and wet.

Overall mean temperatures were close to average in many places, although northern Scotland was colder. The UK mean temperature of 5.7°C was equal to the 1991–2020 average. Rainfall was a different matter; only north-western Scotland received less than normal, with the UK overall 155 per cent wetter than average. It was the sixth wettest March since 1836, and some places in the south of England and Wales saw only half the average amount of sunshine, making it the dullest March since 1910 for some counties.

Rain Shadow
An area to the leeward of high ground, whether hills or mountains, often experiences less rainfall than neighbouring areas or than expected. This rain-shadow effect occurs because as air rises over the higher ground (usually to the west) there is increased rainfall, leaving less moisture to fall on any areas to the leeward of the hills.

Sunrise and Sunset 2025

Location	Date	Rise	Azimuth °	Set	Azimuth °
Belfast					
	1 Mar (Sat)	07:12	102	18:00	259
	11 Mar (Tue)	06:48	95	18:20	265
	21 Mar (Fri)	06:23	88	18:39	272
	31 Mar (Mon)	05:57	81	18:58	279
Cardiff					
	1 Mar (Sat)	06:57	101	17:53	259
	11 Mar (Tue)	06:35	95	18:10	266
	21 Mar (Fri)	06:12	88	18:27	272
	31 Mar (Mon)	05:50	82	18:44	278
Edinburgh					
	1 Mar (Sat)	07:03	102	17:47	258
	11 Mar (Tue)	06:38	95	18:08	265
	21 Mar (Fri)	06:11	88	18:28	272
	31 Mar (Mon)	05:45	81	18:49	279
London					
	1 Mar (Sat)	06:45	101	17:41	259
	11 Mar (Tue)	06:23	95	17:58	266
	21 Mar (Fri)	06:00	88	18:15	272
	31 Mar (Mon)	05:37	82	18:32	278

Note that all times are in Universal Time (UT), otherwise known as Greenwich Mean Time (GMT). These times do not take Summer Time (BST) into account.

Moonrise and Moonset 2025

Location	Date	Rise	Azimuth °	Set	Azimuth °
Belfast					
	1 Mar (Sat)	07:44	91	20:24	276
	11 Mar (Tue)	15:00	59	06:23	304
	21 Mar (Fri)	02:33	144	08:17	215
	31 Mar (Mon)	06:20	60	12:43	307
Cardiff					
	1 Mar (Sat)	07:33	91	20:10	275
	11 Mar (Tue)	15:01	61	05:59	302
	21 Mar (Fri)	01:55	138	06:33	221
	31 Mar (Mon)	06:20	63	22:16	304
Edinburgh					
	1 Mar (Sat)	07:33	91	20:13	276
	11 Mar (Tue)	14:42	58	06:19	306
	21 Mar (Fri)	02:36	147	07:51	213
	31 Mar (Mon)	06:04	59	22:39	309
London					
	1 Mar (Sat)	07:20	91	19:57	275
	11 Mar (Tue)	14:48	61	05:46	302
	21 Mar (Fri)	02:41	138	08:20	221
	31 Mar (Mon)	06:08	63	22:03	304

M

Note that all times are in Universal Time (UT), otherwise known as Greenwich Mean Time (GMT). These times do not take Summer Time (BST) into account.

Twilight Diagrams 2025

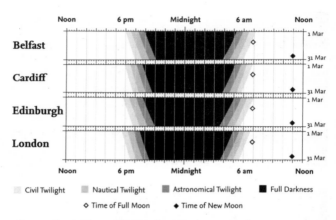

| Civil Twilight | Nautical Twilight | Astronomical Twilight | Full Darkness |

◇ Time of Full Moon   ◆ Time of New Moon

The exact times of the Moon's major phases are shown on the diagrams opposite.

Ferrel cell

One of the two atmospheric circulation cells that are the intermediate cells, between the Hadley cells, closest to the equator, and the polar cells in each hemisphere. The air, spreading out towards the poles from the sub-tropical highs is diverted towards the east by the rotation of the Earth, and forms the dominant westerlies that govern the weather in the middle latitudes.

The Moon's Phases and Ages 2025

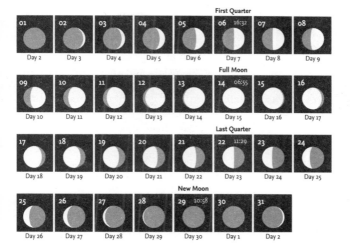

First Quarter

01	02	03	04	05	06 16:32	07	08
Day 2	Day 3	Day 4	Day 5	Day 6	Day 7	Day 8	Day 9

Full Moon

09	10	11	12	13	14 06:55	15	16
Day 10	Day 11	Day 12	Day 13	Day 14	Day 15	Day 16	Day 17

Last Quarter

17	18	19	20	21	22 11:29	23	24
Day 18	Day 19	Day 20	Day 21	Day 22	Day 23	Day 24	Day 25

New Moon

25	26	27	28	29 10:58	30	31
Day 26	Day 27	Day 28	Day 29	Day 30	Day 1	Day 2

M

Hadley cell
One of the two atmospheric circulation cells that are driven by the hot air that rises in the tropics (i.e., along the equator or the heat equator that moves north or south with the seasons). The descending limbs are located over the sub-tropical highs at about latitudes 30° north and south.

March – In This Month

4 March 2019 – Cyclone Idai formed off the east coast of Mozambique. After gradually strengthening over a few days, a period of rapid intensification saw it reach an initial peak intensity on 11 March, and a subsequent peak on 14 March. Altogether, across its two landfalls, it caused severe flooding in Madagascar, Mozambique, Malawi and Zimbabwe, and killed at least 1,500 people. Beira, in central Mozambique saw particularly devastating damage. Damage to infrastructure and sanitation contributed to a cholera outbreak in the storm's aftermath, resulting in further fatalities.

9–13 March 1891 – The Great Blizzard affected southern England, with around 200 people and 6,000 animals killed. The same storm drove the Bay of Panama, a merchant vessel, onto rocks off the Cornish coast, killing 23 people.

10 March 1933 – The Long Beach earthquake struck downtown Los Angeles. Although the epicentre was just offshore, the 6.4-magnitude quake still caused an estimated $40 million of damage to property (equivalent to over $900 million today) and killed over 100 people. In the aftermath, design and construction standards were updated to make new buildings more resistant to earthquakes.

11 March 2011 – The Tōhoku earthquake occurred 72 kilometres east of the Oshika Peninsula. The earthquake's magnitude was 9.0–9.1, and the resulting tsunami caused the Fukushima Daiichi nuclear disaster.

M

13 March 1962 – The Ash Wednesday Storm made landfall in the UK. Although much depleted from the devastating system that had wrought havoc along the eastern seaboard of the USA, it was still strong enough to destroy the seafront at Penzance and damage other nearby villages.

25 March 1948 – The first ever tornado warning made by the US air force. Since then the USA's tornado warning system has developed into a complex network of observation posts, warning sirens and radio and television alerts.

30 March 2010 – A strong late winter storm brought large waves and the highest mean tides of the year to coastal areas in Wales and Scotland. Damage was particularly severe in south-east Scotland, with the City of Edinburgh Council incurring £500,000 of expenses to repair damaged sea defences.

Joanne Simpson

Clouds hold a fascination with many people, whether it's spotting unusual shapes within them or admiring the dramatic sunsets that they help create, but few study them in depth. For Joanne Simpson, they became an integral part of her career. She was the first woman to earn a PhD in Meteorology and her contributions to the field of atmospheric science changed the world of weather for good.

Simpson was born in Boston, Massachusetts, USA, on 23 March 1923. After admiring the clouds while sailing as a little girl, she began to learn about them at the University of Chicago, where she was enlisted as a student pilot during the Second World War. She was fascinated and was soon teaching meteorology to cadets much older than her. After the war, she studied for a PhD, even though the Faculty Advisor told her than no woman had ever got a PhD in Meteorology, and none ever would. During her research, she focused on tropical cumulus clouds. One of her professors advised her that clouds would be a good subject 'for a little girl to study', as no one else in the field was interested in them. Despite not being

Joanne Simpson.

A TRMM scan of a hurricane showing its 'warm core' as predicted by Simpson.

M

taken seriously and facing sexism within the all-male faculty, she went on to receive her PhD in 1949. Her work showed the significance of clouds to the global atmospheric circulation, where previously they were considered an unimportant side-effect of the weather.

In the years that followed, Simpson began to develop an atmospheric model of cumulus clouds at the Woods Hole Oceanographic Institution in Massachusetts. Here, she commissioned the first instrumented aeroplane and proved that heat generated by water condensing within cumulonimbus clouds provides the energy needed to power the global convection patterns known as Hadley cell circulation.

In the 1960s and early 1970s, Simpson led a project that tested cloud seeding as a way of weakening hurricanes before moving to NASA, where she continued developing her cloud models and led the Tropical Rainfall Measuring Mission (TRMM). This culminated in launching the first meteorological radar into space in 1997. She considered this the biggest achievement of her career. It revolutionised scientists' knowledge of the global climate, helping them to estimate the latent heat released by tropical cloud systems, understand how hurricanes develop, and recognise the impact that dust and smoke can have on rainfall.

To this day, Simpson's research has contributed to some of the most important meteorological discoveries, while paving the way for women in weather.

April

Introduction

Known for its flowers and beautiful spring weather, April often brings sunshine and settled conditions. While the rest of the seasons generally see prevailing winds from the south-west, spring tends to buck the trend. For April and May in particular, the frequency of north-easterly winds becomes much higher and is associated with blocking anticyclones developing to the north and west of the country.

Blocking anticyclones are a common feature of the mid-latitudes in the northern hemisphere and cause a disruption to the usual eastward progression of our weather systems. There are two ways in which our weather patterns can become blocked: an omega block and a diffluent block. Omega blocks are named after the Greek letter omega (Ω) due to the shape they form. High pressure develops in the centre, sandwiched by two lows to the east and west. The isobars resulting from this pattern form the distinctive shape that gives the block its name. Diffluent blocks occur when a split in the eastward flow allows high pressure to develop to the north of a low-pressure system.

In either case, blocking typically leads to a prolonged period of settled weather across Britain and Ireland, but not always. If the block develops to the east or west of the country, the UK can be caught in a persistently wet weather pattern, as front after front sweeps through.

While many in the UK remember the April of 2020 for the lockdown during the Covid-19 pandemic, meteorologists will remember the persistently sunny weather that broke records. An average of 223 hours of sunshine was recorded across the UK during the month, while many people were stuck indoors. The record didn't hold for long though, as the following April came along to beat this record by 0.8 hours, thanks to persistent high pressure bringing clear skies and sunshine. Blocking is most likely to develop in the spring but can also lead to extreme heatwaves in the summer and bitter cold in the winter.

The increased likelihood of blocking during this time means April is one of the driest months of the year in the UK, just behind May. This may seem at odds with the well-known phrase, 'April showers bring May flowers'. It helps to remember the difference between frontal rain, which can bring large deluges and lead to flooding, and showers, which tend to be shorter and interspersed with sunshine. The phrase itself originated from a poem written in the sixteenth century by poet and farmer, Thomas Tusser.

Sweete April showers, Forgotten month past,
Doo spring Maie flowers. Doe now at the last.

These showers bring a changeability that characterise Professor Lamb's natural season of 'spring and early summer', spanning from 1 April to 17 June. Where winds blow from the north – as is likely at this time of year – heavy, squally showers may develop, sometimes turning into thunderstorms. As this season progresses, blocking becomes less likely, and is gradually replaced by a feed of moist, maritime air from the west, although depressions are likely to track further north at this time of year.

A

Front
A zone separating two air masses with different characteristics (typically, with different temperatures and/or humidities). Depressions normally show two fronts: a warm front (where warm air is advancing) and a cold front (where cold air is advancing). The latter normally move faster than warm fronts. When a cold front catches up with a warm front, the warm air is lifted away from the surface, giving a pool of warm air at altitude. The combined front is known as an occluded front. Depending on the exact conditions, occluded fronts may give long periods of overcast skies and persistent rain.

Weather Extremes in April

Country	Temp.	Location	Date
Maximum temperature			
England	29.4°C	Camden Square (London)	16 Apr 1949
Wales	26.2°C	Gogerddan (Ceredigion)	16 Apr 2003
Scotland	27.2°C	Inverailort (Highland)	17 Apr 2003
Northern Ireland	24.5°C	Boom Hall (County Londonderry)	26 Apr 1984
Minimum temperature			
England	-15.0°C	Newton Rigg (Cumbria)	2 Apr 1917
Wales	-11.2°C	Corwen (Denbighshire)	11 Apr 1978
Scotland	-15.4°C	Eskdalemuir (Dumfries and Galloway)	2 Apr 1917
Northern Ireland	-8.5°C	Killylane (County Antrim)	10 Apr 1998
Country	**Pressure**	**Location**	**Date**
Maximum pressure			
Scotland	1044.5 hPa	Eskdalemuir (Dumfries and Galloway)	11 Apr 1938
Minimum pressure			
Republic of Ireland	952.9 hPa	Malin Head (County Donegal)	1 Apr 1948

A

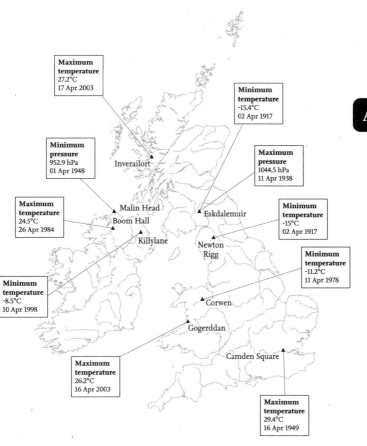

Maximum temperature
27.2°C
17 Apr 2003

Minimum temperature
-15.4°C
02 Apr 1917

Minimum pressure
952.9 hPa
01 Apr 1948

Maximum pressure
1044.5 hPa
11 Apr 1938

Inverailort

Maximum temperature
24.5°C
26 Apr 1984

Malin Head

Boom Hall

Minimum temperature
-15°C
02 Apr 1917

Eskdalemuir

Killylane

Newton Rigg

Minimum temperature
-11.2°C
11 Apr 1978

Minimum temperature
-8.5°C
10 Apr 1998

Corwen

Maximum temperature
26.2°C
16 Apr 2003

Gogerddan

Camden Square

Maximum temperature
29.4°C
16 Apr 1949

The Weather in April 2023

Observation	Location	Date
Max. temperature 21.2°C	Kinlochewe (Ross & Cromarty)	17 April
Min. temperature -7.4°C	Tulloch Bridge (Inverness-shire)	25 April
	Loch Glascarnoch (Ross & Cromarty)	26 April
Most rainfall 54.6 mm	Seathwaite (Cumbria)	11 April
Most sunshine 14.3 hrs	Loch of Hundland (Orkney)	21 April
Highest gust 96 mph (155 kph/83 kt)	Needles Old Battery (Isle of Wight)	12 April

April saw little of note, with weather mostly staying within the parameters of normal for spring. The jet stream was displaced southwards, bringing stronger winds across the south of the UK, with calmer weather further north. However, high pressure was dominant to the east or north of the country for most of the month, meaning any weather systems coming off the Atlantic were fairly weak. Severe weather warnings were sparse and the subdued weather caused relatively low maximum temperatures. Frosts were more common than usual in sheltered areas, and Benson in Oxfordshire saw an overnight low of -5.6°C on the 4th.

The exception to this picture occurred around the middle of the month. On the 11th and 12th a pair of low pressure centres interacted over the UK, bringing strong winds to Wales and southern England. Cairngorm Summit registered gusts of 91 mph (148 kph/127 knots) on the 11th, and the Needles on the Isle of Wight recorded 96 mph (153 kph/83 knots) on the 12th. There were reports of HGVs overturning on the M6 in Cumbria and on the M62 on the border of Greater Manchester and West Yorkshire. Rainfall was also high, with Seathwaite in Cumbria (holder of the UK 24-hour maximum rainfall) recording 54.6 mm. The system was named by MeteoFrance as storm Noa.

The high pressure re-established itself from then on, and southerly winds brought milder temperatures. Kinlochewe in Ross and Cromarty reached 21.2°C on the 17th. Although temperatures fell around the 24th and 25th, the very end of the month saw widespread temperatures in the high teens and low 20s again. The highest minimum of the month was recorded at Castlederg, Tyrone on the 30th, at 11.7°C.

In sum, April was unsettled without being extreme. Temperatures and rainfall fluctuated over the month and between regions, but both averaged around normal overall. Northern Ireland was warmest relative to average, while most of England saw averages slightly below normal. Across the UK, the provisional mean temperature for the month of 7.8°C was 0.1°C below average. Most parts of Scotland were drier than average, but southern and eastern England saw more rainfall than usual. The UK as a whole received 97 per cent of the average rain for the month, and 102 per cent of the average sunshine.

A

Sunrise and Sunset 2025

Location	Date	Rise	Azimuth °	Set	Azimuth °
Belfast					
	1 Apr (Tue)	05:55	81	19:00	280
	11 Apr (Fri)	05:30	74	19:19	286
	21 Apr (Mon)	05:06	68	19:38	293
	30 Apr (Wed)	04:46	62	19:56	298
Cardiff					
	1 Apr (Tue)	05:57	81	18:46	279
	11 Apr (Fri)	05:25	75	19:03	285
	21 Apr (Mon)	05:04	69	19:19	291
	30 Apr (Wed)	04:46	65	19:34	296
Edinburgh					
	1 Apr (Tue)	05:42	80	18:51	280
	11 Apr (Fri)	05:17	74	19:11	287
	21 Apr (Mon)	04:52	67	19:32	293
	30 Apr (Wed)	04:30	61	19:50	299
London					
	1 Apr (Tue)	05:35	81	18:34	279
	11 Apr (Fri)	05:13	75	19:50	285
	21 Apr (Mon)	04:51	69	19:07	291
	30 Apr (Wed)	04:33	65	19:22	296

Note that all times are in Universal Time (UT), otherwise known as Greenwich Mean Time (GMT).

Moonrise and Moonset 2025

Location	Date	Rise	Azimuth °	Set	Azimuth °
Belfast					
	1 Apr (Tue)	06:36	49	–	–
				00:23	317
	11 Apr (Fri)	17:56	97	05:04	268
	21 Apr (Mon)	03:22	134	10:38	228
	30 Apr (Wed)	05:32	37	–	–
				00:46	325
Cardiff					
	1 Apr (Tue)	06:42	53	23:50	313
	11 Apr (Fri)	17:42	97	04:54	268
	21 Apr (Mon)	02:52	131	10:44	232
	30 Apr (Wed)	05:46	42	–	–
				00:06	320
Edinburgh					
	1 Apr (Tue)	06:17	48	–	–
				00:23	319
	11 Apr (Fri)	17:46	98	04:53	268
	21 Apr (Mon)	03:21	136	10:17	226
	30 Apr (Wed)	06:08	35	–	–
				00:50	328
London					
	1 Apr (Tue)	06:29	53	23:37	313
	11 Apr (Fri)	17:29	97	04:41	268
	21 Apr (Mon)	02:39	131	10:31	232
	30 Apr (Wed)	05:34	42	23:54	320

Note that all times are in Universal Time (UT), otherwise known as Greenwich Mean Time (GMT).

Twilight Diagrams 2025

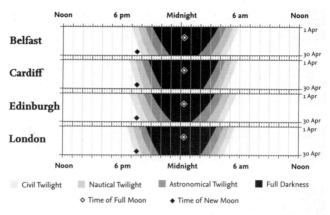

The exact times of the Moon's major phases are shown on the diagrams opposite.

Sub-tropical highs

Semi-permanent areas in both hemispheres around the latitudes of aproximately 30° north and south, where air that has risen at the equator descends back to the surface, becoming heated and dry as it does so. They form the descending limbs of the Hadley cells – the cells closest to the equator.

The Moon's Phases and Ages 2025

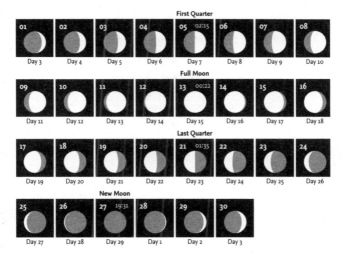

First Quarter

01	02	03	04	05 02:15	06	07	08
Day 3	Day 4	Day 5	Day 6	Day 7	Day 8	Day 9	Day 10

Full Moon

09	10	11	12	13 00:22	14	15	16
Day 11	Day 12	Day 13	Day 14	Day 15	Day 16	Day 17	Day 18

Last Quarter

17	18	19	20	21 01:35	22	23	24
Day 19	Day 20	Day 21	Day 22	Day 23	Day 24	Day 25	Day 26

New Moon

25	26	27 19:31	28	29	30
Day 27	Day 28	Day 29	Day 1	Day 2	Day 3

A

Depression
A low-pressure area. (Often called a 'storm' in North-American
usage.) Winds circulate around a low-pressure centre in an
anticlockwise direction in the northern hemisphere. (Clockwise in
the southern hemisphere.) Away from the surface, and the friction
that it causes, winds flow along the isobars. Depressions generally
move across the globe from west to east, although under certain
conditions they may linger over an area or even (rarely) move
towards the west.

April – In This Month

4 April 2000 – Large parts of England were smothered in snow, with Luton Airport closed and the roads across the Pennines in Derbyshire and South Yorkshire blocked. Further east the precipitation arrived as rain, with flooding reported across the south of England from Cambridgeshire to Somerset.

9–10 April 1998 – Heavy flooding hit the Midlands over the Easter weekend. An area from Worcestershire to the Wash saw over 75 millimetres, and towns including Leamington Spa, Stratford-upon-Avon, Bedford, Northampton and Huntingdon were all flooded. Damage caused by the floods incurred an estimated cost of £50 million, and triggered an independent review into flood-plain management and forecasting.

18 April 1807 – The Harwich Ferry Disaster resulted in the death of between 60 and 90 people when a ferry overloaded with passengers (mainly soldiers and their families) was caught in a strong wind and capsized.

18 April 1849 – A large snowstorm engulfed Britain. Travel and communication networks were damaged, while farmers worried for their livestock and crops. The *Inverness Courier* reported that 'the lambs are fast appearing and equally fast vanishing again. Hardly half of them live above a few hours due to the cold easterly wind and snow.'

19 April 2018 – St James's Park in London recorded a
temperature of 28.1°C, the hottest April day since 1949. The
1949 reading is unreliable, however, so 2018 may well have seen
the highest April temperature since records began.

24–29 April 1916 – The Easter Rising saw Irish republicans
launch an armed rebellion against British rule in Ireland. The
uprising was helped by favourable weather, although a more
detailed study of the weather's impact is not possible, because
the normal daily weather observations made at Trinity College
Dublin were not taken 'owing to disturbances in Dublin'.

28 April 1902 – Léon Teisserenc de Bort announced the
discovery of the stratosphere. He noticed that in this portion
of the atmosphere, which begins at an altitude of about 11 km,
temperatures first stabilise, then begin to increase with height.
See page 147 for a fuller explanation of this.

TIROS-1

The TIROS-1 satellite.

On 1 April 1960 a satellite was launched which changed the future of weather forecasting forever. The Television Infrared Observation Satellite (TIROS) Program, coordinated by NASA, aimed to determine whether satellites could be useful in the study of the Earth, and TIROS-1 became the world's first weather satellite. TIROS-1 was a spacecraft just over 1 metre wide, composed of aluminium alloy and stainless steel, and covered in solar cells to keep its batteries charged. It housed two television cameras which, for the first time, provided meteorologists with detailed pictures of the clouds on Earth from above. TIROS-1 orbited from pole to pole, capturing an image of the planet below every 30 seconds. It was operational for 78 days, and in that time, sent back 19,389 usable pictures to forecasters, proving just how useful a weather satellite could be.

The TIROS Program was extremely successful, and over the next five years, NASA launched nine successors to TIROS-1, each with various changes and improvements on the last. By 1962, the TIROS Program was able to provide continuous coverage of the Earth's weather, helping to deliver the first accurate weather forecasts based on data from space. Various weather satellite programs followed the success of TIROS in the USA, including the NIMBUS Series, the ESSA and NOAA polar orbiting satellites, the GOES Network, and many more.

Up until the mid-1970s, satellites operated in the same way as TIROS-1, orbiting pole to pole. In 1974, the first geostationary weather satellite, SMS-1, was launched. It led the way for the GOES (Geostationary Operational Environmental Satellites) Project, which launched the following year. These satellites orbit the planet at the same speed as the Earth's rotation, so while every image from the TIROS spacecrafts captured a slightly different location, the SMS and GOES craft were able to provide images of the same area over time. This program is still operational today, with the launch of GOES-U in 2024.

Modern satellites continue to innovate. In December 2022, the European Organisation for the Exploitation of Meteorological Satellites (EUMETSAT), launched the first of its new generation of geostationary satellites – MTG-I1. The imagery from this satellite is of a much higher resolution than its predecessors and it also has a new instrument on board – a Lightning Imager – helping meteorologists to observe severe thunderstorms. The next satellite to be launched in this project is a 'sounder', which will provide a full profile of the atmosphere at multiple altitudes – the type of data usually gathered by a weather balloon.

A

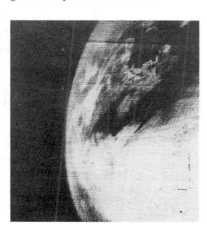

The first television picture of Earth from space, taken by TIROS-1 on 1 April 1960.

Anticyclone
A high-pressure area. Winds circulate around anticyclones in a clockwise direction in the northern hemisphere. (Anticlockwise in the southern hemisphere.) Anticyclones are slow-moving systems (unlike depressions) and tend to extend their influence slowly from an existing centre.

May

Introduction

May continues on a similar path to April. It is typically a drier and more settled month compared to the rest of the year but can still be changeable. Thunderstorm activity generally increases through this month and can even begin to be imported from the European continent. May 2021 was notably thundery across the UK, and frequent downpours contributed to the month's high rainfall totals too, making it the second wettest May on record, following May 1967.

Historically, May is the earliest month of the year in which temperatures have exceeded 30°C. The warmest May day on record was 29 May 1944, when the mercury soared to 32.8°C in West Sussex, Kent and London. High pressure centred to the south of Scandinavia brought a south-easterly feed of hot and dry continental air across Britain and Ireland, with clear skies and bright sunshine over southern England. The heat was eventually broken as thunderstorms developed in the south. Archived forecasts and observations from the Met Office during this time are marked 'SECRET', as this was a crucial time in the ongoing Second World War. Just over a week later, meteorologists predicted the window of weather that allowed the successful D-Day landings.

Although temperatures are increasing through May, as days lengthen and summer approaches, frosts are still possible. Grass or ground frosts are more likely than air frosts, as these can occur even if air temperatures remain above freezing, since the ground cools more quickly than the air. Gardeners will be keeping a keen eye out for the risk of grass frost during late spring and early summer, as well as viticulturists, whose grapevines are going into bud break. The buds are protected from the cold in winter, but once warmer weather arrives and they have burst, they are much more vulnerable. In fact, in May 2020, one Sussex-based vineyard reported losing more than 80 per cent of their crop due to harsh, late frosts. When frost is forecast, it's not unusual to see fires or candles lit around vineyards, in an attempt to keep temperatures up.

This reputation that May can bring late frosts is no doubt the reason behind the saying, 'Ne'er cast a clout till May be out'. Decipher this phrase from its Old English origins and the message is clear – don't put away your winter clothes until the end of May!

In May, the Full Moon is aptly named the 'Flower Moon', after the colourful blooms that spring up during this month. It is also known as the 'Blossom Moon', 'Corn-planting Moon', or 'Mothers' Moon', the latter named after the animals who are busy looking after their young at this time of year.

M

Synoptic
The term 'synoptic' is used extensively in meteorology to indicate that the data used in preparing a chart (for example) were all obtained at the same time and thus show the state of the atmosphere at a particular moment.

Weather Extremes in May

Country	Temp.	Location	Date
Maximum temperature			
England	32.8°C	Camden Square (London)	22 May 1922
		Horsham (West Sussex)	29 May 1944
		Tunbridge Wells (Kent)	29 May 1944
		Regent's Park (London)	29 May 1944
Wales	30.6°C	Newport (Monmouthshire)	29 May 1944
Scotland	30.9°C	Inverailort (Highland)	25 May 2012
Northern Ireland	28.3°C	Lisburn (County Antrim)	31 May 1922
Minimum temperature			
England	-9.4°C	Lynford (Norfolk)	4 May 1941
			11 May 1941
Wales	-6.2°C	St Harmon (Powys)	14 May 2020
Scotland	-8.8°C	Braemar (Aberdeenshire)	1 May 1927
Northern Ireland	-6.5°C	Moydamlaght (County Londonderry)	7 May 1982

Country	Pressure	Location	Date
Maximum pressure			
Republic of Ireland	1043.0 hPA	Sherkin Island (County Cork) Valentia Observatory (County Kerry)	12 May 2012
Minimum pressure			
England	968.0 hPa	Sealand (Cheshire)	8 May 1943

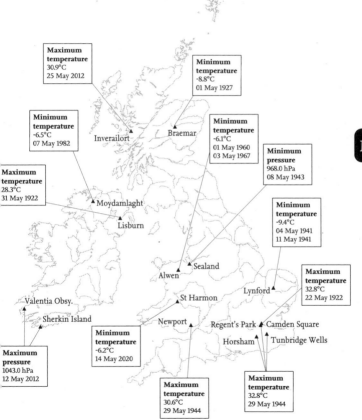

Maximum temperature
30.9°C
25 May 2012

Minimum temperature
-8.8°C
01 May 1927

Minimum temperature
-6.5°C
07 May 1982

Inverailort

Braemar

Minimum temperature
-6.1°C
01 May 1960
03 May 1967

Minimum pressure
968.0 hPa
08 May 1943

Maximum temperature
28.3°C
31 May 1922

Moydamlaght

Lisburn

Minimum temperature
-9.4°C
04 May 1941
11 May 1941

Alwen

Sealand

Maximum temperature
32.8°C
22 May 1922

Valentia Obsy.

St Harmon

Lynford

Sherkin Island

Newport

Regent's Park

Camden Square

Maximum pressure
1043.0 hPa
12 May 2012

Minimum temperature
-6.2°C
14 May 2020

Horsham

Tunbridge Wells

Maximum temperature
30.6°C
29 May 1944

Maximum temperature
32.8°C
29 May 1944

M

The Weather in May 2023

Observation	Location	Date
Max. temperature 25.1°C	Porthmadog (Gwynedd)	30 May
Min. temperature -2.2°C	Loch Glascarnoch (Ross & Cromarty)	2 May
Most rainfall 43.6 mm	Harestock Sewage Works (Hampshire)	9 May
Most sunshine 16.2 hrs	Tiree (Argyll)	30 May
Highest gust 62 mph (100 kph/54 kt	Warkop Range (Cumbria)	4 May

May saw generally settled weather, with the exception of scattered thunderstorms in the second week. Locally intense downpours on the 5th resulted in surface flooding in Lincolnshire, and from the 7th severe weather warnings were issued for much of southern and central England. The 9th saw severe showers and thunderstorms develop, starting in south-western England and the south coast. Harestock in Hampshire saw 43.6 millimetres of rain. Flooding caused problems in villages across Devon, while in North Cadbury, Somerset, evacuated residents sheltered in the village hall. In Hampshire a landslip caused a railway closure, while in Essex a section of the M11 was closed due to flooding.

Over the following two days the rain spread to the Midlands, Wales, London and East Anglia, with reports of floods in Stevenage and elsewhere across Hertfordshire on the 11th. Some rain continued over the next few days and temperatures remained low, with frosts reported in all regions as late as the 16th.

The rest of the month was a good deal drier, driven by a weak jet stream and an extended area of high pressure across the UK for much of the period. Barring a band of rain that swept across Scotland and Northern Ireland on the 20th, very little rain fell at all from the 15th onwards. As the ground dried out, wildfires were reported across Wales on the 21st and 22nd, and in the last week of the month there were further fires reported from Dartmoor in the south-west to Marsden Moor in West Yorkshire. By the end of the month maximum temperatures had breached 25.1°C at Porthmadog in Gwynedd, and all parts of the UK saw at least one day with at least 15 hours of sunshine.

Overall, the settled, anticyclonic conditions meant a drier and warmer month than average. The mean temperature for the UK was 1°C above average, at 11.6°C, and parts of Scotland were considerably warmer than normal. Sunshine was at 108 per cent of average, with western England and Wales receiving more sun than northern and eastern areas. Although the south of England from Devon to Norfolk saw marginally above average rainfall, much of the northern and western UK was far drier than normal, and the country overall received just 55 per cent of its average rain.

M

Sunrise and Sunset 2025

Location	Date	Rise	Azimuth °	Set	Azimuth °
Belfast					
	1 May (Thu)	04:44	62	19:58	298
	11 May (Sun)	04:24	56	20:16	304
	21 May (Wed)	04:08	52	20:33	308
	31 May (Sat)	03:55	48	20:47	312
Cardiff					
	1 May (Thu)	04:44	64	19:36	296
	11 May (Sun)	04:26	59	19:52	301
	21 May (Wed)	04:12	55	20:06	308
	31 May (Sat)	03:55	48	20:48	305
Edinburgh					
	1 May (Thu)	04:28	61	19:52	300
	11 May (Sun)	04:07	55	20:12	305
	21 May (Wed)	03:49	50	20:30	310
	31 May (Sat)	03:36	48	20:45	314
London					
	1 May (Thu)	04:32	64	19:24	296
	11 May (Sun)	04:14	59	19:40	301
	21 May (Wed)	04:00	55	19:54	305
	31 May (Sat)	03:49	52	20:07	308

Note that all times are in Universal Time (UT), otherwise known as Greenwich Mean Time (GMT). These times do not take Summer Time (BST) into account.

Moonrise and Moonset 2025

Location	Date	Rise	Azimuth °	Set	Azimuth °
Belfast					
	1 May (Thu)	06:25	35	00:46	325
	11 May (Sun)	19:31	124	03:34	242
	21 May (Wed)	02:06	108	12:45	257
	31 May (Sat)	08:08	50	00:40	313
Cardiff					
	1 May (Thu)	06:41	40	00:06	320
	11 May (Sun)	19:05	121	03:34	244
	21 May (Wed)	01:49	107	12:38	258
	31 May (Sat)	08:14	53	00:11	310
Edinburgh					
	1 May (Thu)	05:58	32	00:50	328
	11 May (Sun)	19:26	125	03:18	241
	21 May (Wed)	01:58	109	12:31	257
	31 May (Sat)	07:48	48	00:38	315
London					
	1 May (Thu)	06:28	40	–	–
				00:53	319
	11 May (Sun)	18:53	121	03:21	244
	21 May (Wed)	01:36	107	12:25	258
	31 May (Sat)	08:01	53	–	–
				00:20	302

Note that all times are in Universal Time (UT), otherwise known as Greenwich Mean Time (GMT). These times do not take Summer Time (BST) into account.

Twilight Diagrams 2025

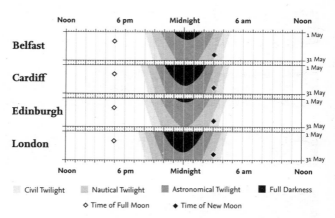

The exact times of the Moon's major phases are shown on the diagrams opposite.

Adiabatic

Any process in which heat does not enter or leave the system.
Air rising in the troposphere generally cools at an adiabatic
rate, because it does not lose heat to its surroundings. The fall
in temperature is solely because of its expansion: its increase
in volume, because of the decrease in pressure with increasing
altitude.

The Moon's Phases and Ages 2025

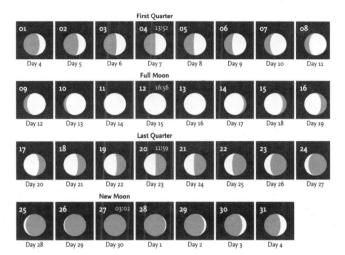

First Quarter

01	02	03	04 13:52	05	06	07	08
Day 4	Day 5	Day 6	Day 7	Day 8	Day 9	Day 10	Day 11

Full Moon

09	10	11	12 16:56	13	14	15	16
Day 12	Day 13	Day 14	Day 15	Day 16	Day 17	Day 18	Day 19

Last Quarter

17	18	19	20 11:59	21	22	23	24
Day 20	Day 21	Day 22	Day 23	Day 24	Day 25	Day 26	Day 27

New Moon

25	26	27 03:02	28	29	30	31
Day 28	Day 29	Day 30	Day 1	Day 2	Day 3	Day 4

Azores High
A more-or-less permanent high-pressure system in the North Atlantic, generally centred approximately over the islands of the Azores, or closer to Iberia (Portugal and Spain). It arises from air that has risen at the equator that descends at the sub-tropical high-pressure zones.

May – In This Month

7 May 2018 – A high of 28.7°C at London Northolt made this the warmest early May bank holiday on record since the holiday was introduced in 1978.

9 May 1785 – James Pollard Espy was born. Nicknamed the 'Storm King', he developed the modern convection theory of storms and also proposed early ideas for climate engineering.

11 May 1985 – A fire broke out at Bradford City Stadium during a match between Bradford and Lincoln. The windy conditions meant the whole stand was engulfed within minutes, and 56 people were killed.

14 May 1992 – Edinburgh recorded a high of 29°C in what marked the peak of the warmest May of the century. Later in the month saw rain and hail storms, but high temperatures returned over the late spring bank holiday, with 27°C recorded at Southampton and 28.2°C at Norwich.

18 May 2020 – A wildfire started in Wareham Forest in Dorset. Thought to have been caused by a disposable barbecue or campfire, the blaze lasted several days, with multiple smaller flareups continuing after the main fire had been extinguished.

20 May 1514 – Trinity House Corporation was founded by royal charter, following a petition by Deptford-based mariners for Thames pilots to be regulated. The corporation is responsible for lighthouses and other navigational aids in English and Welsh waters, as well as being a pilotage authority operating across Northern Europe.

20 May 1729 – A waterspout made landfall at Bexhill in East Sussex. This followed several days of stifling weather and was described in detail by local resident Richard Budgen, who was keeping a daily weather journal at the time. Once over land, the width of the tornado reached up to 300 metres, causing extensive damage to woodland and houses. The records made by Budgen include one of the first uses of the word 'tornado' in its modern sense, and the earliest known printed map of a tornado track.

M

23 May 1917 – American mathematician and meteorologist Edward Norton Lorenz was born. Lorenz established the principle of using statistical models to predict climate and weather patterns, and pioneered computer-aided atmospheric physics. In mathematics, he is the founder of modern chaos theory.

27 May 1774 – Birth of Francis Beaufort; he went on to develop the Beaufort Scale for wind force.

31 May 2020 – A new UK record for the number of hours of sunshine in a month was set. That May saw an average of 266 hours of sunshine across the UK, 143 per cent of average, and the country received less than half the average expected rainfall. The spring months in total saw 626 hours of sunshine, surpassing the previous record for the sunniest spring by 70 hours.

The First Greenhouse Effect Calculation

The term 'Greenhouse Effect' was first described in 1824 by French mathematician Joseph Fourier, who compared the Earth's atmosphere to the glass of a greenhouse. It relates to the warming effect created by the presence of 'greenhouse gases' in the atmosphere. These gases, including water vapour, carbon dioxide and methane, are naturally present in our atmosphere and are essential to life on Earth. When energy from the Sun reaches the Earth's surface, much of it is reflected as infrared radiation. However, greenhouse gases trap this energy, raising the temperature of the atmosphere. Without them, the Earth's average surface temperature would be about -18°C.

You can have too much of a good thing though. The industrial revolution caused the amount of greenhouse gases in the atmosphere to increase, and the resultant warming effect is causing global climate change.

Through the 1900s, concern began to grow about the increasing levels of greenhouse gases. Many scientists tried and failed to produce accurate models of the Earth's atmosphere. A pivotal moment came with the publication of the first accurate greenhouse effect calculation on 1 May 1967, by climate scientists Syukuro Manabe and Richard Wetherald. For the first time, the effect of convection within the atmosphere was considered, and the result was a model that was much closer to real-world observations.

Within their 1967 study, Manabe and Wetherald imagined a world in which the amount of carbon dioxide in the atmosphere had doubled from current levels. They found that this would lead to a global warming of around 2°C. Considering it was the first accurate prediction of future temperature rise, and calculations have become much more complex since, it has stood the test of time remarkably well. It's not far off the most recent projections from the Intergovernmental Panel on Climate Change, which predicts a temperature rise anywhere between 1.9°C and 8.5°C by the end of this century, depending on the amount of greenhouse gas emissions. It is, perhaps, for this reason that many scientists consider it to be one of the most influential studies of all time.

M

Syukuro Manabe was awarded the Nobel Prize in Physics for his work.

June

Introduction

The word 'summer' often brings to mind long hazy days, crowded beaches and dripping ice creams. Although June marks the start of meteorological summer, it doesn't necessarily mean settled weather. In fact, June 2012 was the wettest and dullest on record, receiving twice its average rainfall and only 113 hours of sunshine, compared to an average of 171 hours. The month often brings a 'return of the westerlies' and has even been dubbed the 'European Monsoon'. It is, of course, not technically a monsoon but a shift in prevailing winds and a resultant change in weather conditions. The phrase 'return of the westerlies' was coined by Professor Lamb in his 1950 paper describing seasonal changes across the British Isles. He found that, following more north-easterly dominated weather in April and May, the winds would return to a westerly direction around mid-June.

This change marks the start of the 'high summer' season, from 18 June to 9 September, defined by dominant westerly winds and accompanying depressions, interspersed with periods of more settled, anticyclonic conditions bringing warmth and sunshine. These drier spells present perfect opportunities for cutting hay, which must be left out to dry for several days. Accurate weather forecasts are a farmer's greatest friend during this time, but even so, they will probably be anxiously refreshing their weather apps to check for rain!

Only a few days after the start of high summer is the summer solstice, falling on 21 June in 2025, which marks the beginning of astronomical summer. Earth is tilted on its axis, and for the UK, the summer solstice occurs when the northern hemisphere is most tilted towards the Sun, giving this day the highest number of daylight hours. In winter, the opposite occurs, with the winter solstice occurring when the northern hemisphere is tilted furthest away from the Sun.

At the summer solstice, the Sun is at its highest point in the sky and because of this, sunlight has less atmosphere to travel through before it reaches us. Thus, ultraviolet radiation (UV) levels are at their peak, though the amount of cloud in the troposphere (where all our weather happens) and the amount of ozone in the stratosphere also affect the precise level.

The sixth Full Moon of 2025 will be June's 'Strawberry Moon', also known as the 'Rose Moon'. These names do not refer to the colour of the Moon, although if it fell at the same time as a lunar eclipse, it would indeed appear pinky red in colour. Instead, the 'Strawberry Moon' is thought to have originated from Native American tribes, who used it to mark the beginning of strawberry harvesting season in North America. Meanwhile, in medieval Europe, it was referred to as the 'Mead Moon', which heralded the time that meadows were mown, hay was collected and mead was made.

Noctilucent Clouds

Clouds visible in the night sky during midsummer, in the general direction of the North Pole for observers in northern latitudes. The name means 'night-shining', and these clouds are seen when the observer is in darkness but the clouds are still illuminated by the sun below the horizon. This is possible because these clouds are the highest in the atmosphere at about 85 kilometres (most 'normal' clouds do not extend above an altitude of 20 kilometres). They consist of ice crystals, believed to form around meteoric dust arriving from space. They also occur in the southern hemisphere, but due to the distribution of landmasses are normally only visible from the Antarctic Peninsula.

Weather Extremes in June

Country	Temp.	Location	Date
Maximum temperature			
England	35.6°C	Camden Square (London)	29 Jun 1957
		Mayflower Park (Southampton)	28 Jun 1976
Wales	33.7°C	Machynlleth (Powys)	18 Jun 2000
Scotland	32.2°C	Ochtertyre (Perth & Kinross)	18 Jun 1893
Northern Ireland	30.8°C	Knockarevan (County Fermanagh)	30 Jun 1976
Minimum temperature			
England	-5.6°C	Santon Downham (Norfolk)	1 Jun 1962 3 Jun 1962
Wales	-4.0°C	St Harmon (Powys)	8 Jun 1985
Scotland	-5.6°C	Dalwhinnie (Highland)	9 Jun 1955
Northern Ireland	-2.4°C	Lough Navar Forest (County Fermanagh)	4 Jun 1991

Country	Pressure	Location	Date
Maximum pressure			
Republic of Ireland	1043.1 hPa	Clones (County Monaghan)	14 Jun 1959
Minimum pressure			
Scotland	968.4 hPa	Lerwick (Shetland)	28 Jun 1938

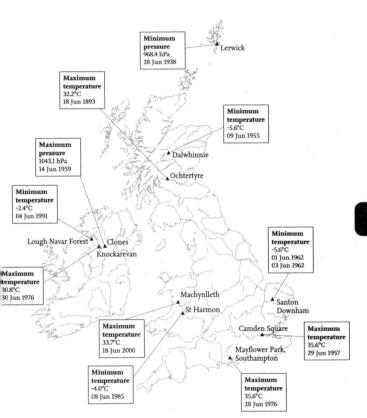

Minimum pressure
968.4 hPa
28 Jun 1938
Lerwick

Maximum temperature
32.2°C
18 Jun 1893

Minimum temperature
-5.6°C
09 Jun 1955

Dalwhinnie

Ochtertyre

Maximum pressure
1043.1 hPa
14 Jun 1959

Minimum temperature
-2.4°C
04 Jun 1991

Minimum temperature
-5.6°C
01 Jun 1962
03 Jun 1962

Lough Navar Forest   Clones
Knockarevan

Maximum temperature
30.8°C
30 Jun 1976

Machynlleth
St Harmon

Santon Downham

Camden Square

Maximum temperature
33.7°C
18 Jun 2000

Mayflower Park, Southampton

Maximum temperature
35.6°C
29 Jun 1957

Minimum temperature
-4.0°C
08 Jun 1985

Maximum temperature
35.6°C
28 Jun 1976

J

The Weather in June 2023

Observation	Location	Date
Max. temperature 32.2°C	Chertsey, Abbey Mead (Surrey)	10 June
	Coningsby (Lincolnshire)	25 June
Min. temperature -2.6°C	Kinbrace (Sutherland)	2 June
Most rainfall 70.4 mm	Wiley Sike No. 2 (Cumbria)	18 June
Most sunshine 16.9 hrs	Loch of Hundland (Orkney)	15 June
Highest gust 54 mph (47 kt)	South Uist Range (Western Isles)	24 June

The month began uneventfully, with the settled anticyclonic conditions continuing. As the high pressure moved away, warm continental air affected all parts, with mean, maximum and minimum temperature records broken in all regions. Highs exceeded 32°C in Surrey on the 10th.

More humid air brought rain and thunderstorms in the West Midlands and north-west England. Rain spread over the next two days, and on the 13th flooding was reported from London to as far north as Inverness. Flash floods closed the M6 for a short period, and the West Highland Line between Fort William and Crianlarich was closed for several days. In addition, landslides closed several roads in Scotland. Many places in the east of England had seen almost no rainfall by this point in the month, however.

The following few days were more settled but still very warm before more convective systems developing from the Atlantic brought thundery downpours across the whole of the UK between the 16th and the 22nd. Houses were flooded in Radcliffe, Greater Manchester, and roads and properties impacted from Norfolk to Devon. Wiley Sike (the bombing range at Spadeadam in Cumbria) received 70.4 mm of rain on the 18th. There were delays on the West Coast Main Line between London and Liverpool on the 20th, and the 22nd brought disruption to rail services in the Glasgow area.

The rest of the month remained changeable but humidity and high temperatures dominated, with Coningsby in Lincolnshire recording a maximum of 32.2°C on the 25th. More rain brought some respite from the heat, with temperatures everywhere much cooler from the 26th to the end of the month, but humidity remained high.

Overall, this was the warmest June since 1884 and the sunniest since 1957, with the UK mean temperature for the month 2.5°C higher than average. Unprecedented warm, humid weather saw maxima in excess of 25°C for over a fortnight. Average temperatures were exceeded in all areas, with parts of western Scotland seeing mean maximum temperatures reach 4°C above average. It was almost the warmest June globally on record, beating the record from 2019. Although the northwest and parts of the Midlands received slightly above average rainfall, Wales, the south and the east were very dry, and as a whole the UK received only 68 per cent of its average rainfall.

J

Sunrise and Sunset 2025

Location	Date	Rise	Azimuth °	Set	Azimuth °
Belfast					
	1 Jun (Sun)	03:54	48	20:49	312
	11 Jun (Wed)	03:48	46	20:59	314
	21 Jun (Sat)	03:47	45	21:03	315
	30 Jun (Mon)	03:51	46	21:03	314
Cardiff					
	1 Jun (Sun)	04:01	52	20:20	309
	11 Jun (Wed)	03:55	50	20:29	310
	21 Jun (Sat)	03:55	49	20:33	311
	30 Jun (Mon)	03:59	49	20:33	310
Edinburgh					
	1 Jun (Sun)	03:34	46	20:47	314
	11 Jun (Wed)	03:27	44	20:57	316
	21 Jun (Sat)	03:26	43	21:02	317
	30 Jun (Mon)	03:30	44	21:01	316
London					
	1 Jun (Sun)	03:48	52	20:08	309
	11 Jun (Wed)	03:43	50	20:17	310
	21 Jun (Sat)	03:43	49	20:21	311
	30 Jun (Mon)	03:47	49	20:21	310

Note that all times are in Universal Time (UT), otherwise known as Greenwich Mean Time (GMT). These times do not take Summer Time (BST) into account.

Moonrise and Moonset 2025

Location	Date	Rise	Azimuth °	Set	Azimuth °
Belfast					
	1 Jun (Sun)	09:36	59	00:57	304
	11 Jun (Wed)	22:12	145	02:58	216
	21 Jun (Sat)	00:49	65	16:31	302
	30 Jun (Mon)	09:58	76	23:31	278
Cardiff					
	1 Jun (Sun)	09:37	62	00:32	301
	11 Jun (Wed)	21:32	140	03:13	221
	21 Jun (Sat)	00:47	67	16:06	299
	30 Jun (Mon)	09:52	77	–	–
				00:17	277
Edinburgh					
	1 Jun (Sun)	09:19	58	00:52	305
	11 Jun (Wed)	22:16	148	02:32	313
	21 Jun (Sat)	00:33	53	16:25	303
	30 Jun (Mon)	09:44	76	23:21	278
London					
	1 Jun (Sun)	09:24	62	00:20	302
	11 Jun (Wed)	21:20	140	03:00	221
	21 Jun (Sat)	00:34	67	15:53	288
	30 Jun (Mon)	09:39	77	23:05	277

J

Note that all times are in Universal Time (UT), otherwise known as Greenwich Mean Time (GMT). These times do not take Summer Time (BST) into account.

Twilight Diagrams 2025

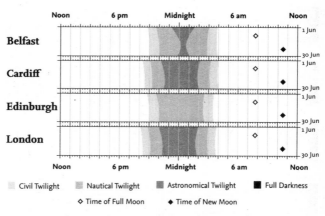

The exact times of the Moon's major phases are shown on the diagrams opposite.

Troposphere

The lowest layer in the atmosphere, in which essentially all weather occurs. It is defined by the way in which temperature declines with height, and is bounded at the top by the tropopause (an inversion at which temperatures either stabilise or begin to increase with height in the overlying stratosphere). The height of the tropopause (and thus the depth of the troposphere) increases from about 7 kilometres at the poles to 14–18 kilometres at the equator.

The Moon's Phases and Ages 2025

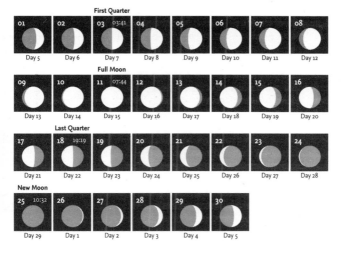

Tropopause

The tropopause is the boundary between the lowest layer in the atmosphere (the troposphere) and the next highest (the stratosphere). It is an inversion at which temperatures either stabilise or begin to increase with height in the overlying stratosphere. The height of the tropopause (and thus the depth of the troposphere) increases from about 7 kilometres at the poles to 14–18 kilometres at the equator. There are breaks in the level of the 145 (particularly near the location of jet streams) and these do allow some exchange of air between the layers.

June – In This Month

12 June 1953 – Queen Elizabeth II's coronation took place on a cold and damp day. There were highs of just 11.8°C and persistent light rain. Whereas May had been warm and sunny, with 31.7°C recorded on the Whitsun bank holiday, the first week of June was dominated by a chilly northerly airflow. At least the coronation didn't happen further north, where torrential rain caused flooding and temperatures were even colder.

3 June 2012 – The pageant on the River Thames for the Queen's diamond jubilee was beset by heavy rain. The wet conditions continued through the month, with flooding in Wales and the south coast, followed by Lancashire and Cumbria, over the next few weeks.

7 June 1861 – The British merchant ship *Prince of Wales* ran aground on the Brazilian coast *en route* to Argentina, with no survivors. The wreck sparked a diplomatic row between the UK and Brazil, with the latter accused of stealing cargo from the beached ship.

14 June 1931 – A tornado caused damage in the Sparkbrook and Erdington areas of Birmingham, with one person killed.

16 June 1917 – A severe thunderstorm delivered 118 millimetres of rain in 2 hours at Kensington in London.

21 June 1919 – The German fleet was scuttled while at anchor in Scapa Flow. Although some of the ships were re-floated, many remain on the seabed and are a popular destination for scuba divers, as well as an important source of low-background steel (that is, steel produced before the detonation of the first nuclear bombs, and therefore uncontaminated by radioactive isotopes).

24 June 2005 – The start of the Glastonbury music festival was badly disrupted by torrential rain. After a week-long heatwave, thunderstorms brought flash floods, with tents submerged after a river burst its banks.

24 June 2018 – The Saddleworth Moor fire started. It went on to burn for over three weeks, destroying over 18 sq. kilometres of moorland.

The Battle of Waterloo

The weather affects our lives every day. From the clothes we put on in the morning, to the foods we eat and how we travel. But in June 1815, it may well have changed the course of history. This was the belief of *Les Misérables* author, Victor Hugo, who wrote:

> *'If it had not rained on the night of June 17, 1815, the future of Europe would have been different. A few drops more or less tipped the balance against Napoleon. For Waterloo to be the end of Austerlitz, Providence needed only a little rain, and an unseasonable cloud crossing the sky was enough for the collapse of a world.'*

He is of course referring to the Battle of Waterloo, which was fought on Sunday, 18 June 1815. Heavy rain had fallen on the previous day and overnight, leading to waterlogged grounds and a delay in the start of the battle. Some historians believe that it gave Wellington's army of British, German and Dutch troops time to gather and rally against the French, ultimately leading to their victory and Napoleon's downfall.

The rain has been put down to a series of fronts and an associated low pressure system, which moved across the battle area on 16 and 17 June, followed by violent thunderstorms. Yet perhaps a larger influence was at play too. It is well known that volcanic eruptions can impact the weather and climate. Just a few months prior to the Battle of Waterloo, Mount Tambora unleashed the largest recorded volcanic eruption in recent history. It spewed clouds of ash and volcanic gases high into the atmosphere, including around 200 million tonnes of sulphur dioxide. High up in the stratosphere, this gas combines with water vapour to form tiny droplets of sulphuric acid – reflecting incoming solar radiation. Ash and dust particles can also have a similar effect of reducing the amount of solar radiation that reaches Earth's surface, but sulphuric acid can persist in the atmosphere for much longer – up to three years. This combination of effects often leads to a temporary cooling of the planet, sometimes known as a 'volcanic winter'. In fact, the year after the eruption of Mount Tambora and the Battle of Waterloo was known as 'the year without a summer'.

Some scientists believe that the eruption may also have contributed to increased cloud formation and rainfall in the months following the event. Scientific theories suggest that rainfall is supressed immediately after an eruption, leading to increased atmospheric water content. Therefore, once normal cloud formation resumes, both cloud cover and precipitation increase. This could explain why the months of May and June in 1815 were so wet across Europe and may even have affected the outcome of the Battle of Waterloo itself.

The Battle of Waterloo *(detail) by William Allan.*

J

July

Introduction

July brings the height of British summertime. It is, on average, the hottest month of the year, and is also most likely to bring the hottest day of the year. You would be forgiven for thinking that June ought to have the hottest temperatures, as this is the month in which the Sun is highest in the sky, but a seasonal lag generally means it happens later. Although the air warms and cools with the Sun relatively quickly, the oceans, which have a high thermal capacity (the amount of heat energy required to cause a given rise in temperature), take much longer to react.

This is similar to a pot of water being heated on the stove; if you bring it to a gradual boil and towards the end of the process, turn the heat down, the water temperature will continue to rise. In June, the oceans are still relatively cold, but by July have warmed enough that they start to heat the air in return, driving overall temperatures to their maximum.

Combining this with long hours of sunshine, July often sees heatwaves. The Met Office defines a heatwave as three consecutive days where maximum temperatures reach a certain temperature threshold, and this is different depending on where you are in the country. July 2022 saw the hottest day on record, and the first time temperatures in the UK reached, and exceeded 40°C. Scientists say this extreme temperature would not have been possible if it wasn't for human-induced climate change.

As our climate changes and global temperatures increase, heatwaves are becoming more extreme and frequent. Since a warmer atmosphere can hold more moisture, extreme rainfall is also increasing. In July 2021, London was hit twice by flash flooding. This is when rain falls so quickly that the ground cannot drain it away fast enough. On 12 July, an official weather station at Kew Gardens recorded one month's worth of rain within just a few hours, while there were reports of up to 100 millimetres of rain falling in Hammersmith. Between them, London Fire Brigade and Thames Water received more than 3,500 calls about the floods. Thirteen days later, London was hit again. A total of 41.8 millimetres of rain fell at St James's Park. Eight underground stations were closed, patients were evacuated from hospitals, and houses were filled with stormwater and sewage.

Both events were also accompanied by frequent lightning, a common feature in July. Three ingredients are required for thunderstorms: instability, lift and moisture. When temperature declines with height in the atmosphere, it is considered unstable. Lift can be provided in a few ways – the Sun heating the air near the ground, orographic lift, or instability within a front. As mentioned previously, warm air can hold more moisture than cool air, but the source of this air also matters, as maritime air is naturally very moist, while continental air is drier.

J

Orographic
A term used to describe rain or other conditions that arise when air is forced to rise over high ground. The increase of rainfall (orographic rain) is a common occurrence over the mountains of Wales and Scotland.

Weather Extremes in July

Country	Temp.	Location	Date
Maximum temperature			
England	40.3°C	Coningsby (Lincolnshire)	19 Jul 2022
Wales	37.1°C	Hawarden Airport (Flintshire)	18 Jul 2022
Scotland	34.8°C	Charterhall (Scottish Borders)	19 Jul 2022
Northern Ireland	31.3°C	Castlederg (County Tyrone)	21 Jul 2021
Minimum temperature			
England	-1.7°C	Kielder Castle (Northumberland)	17 Jul 1965
Wales	-1.5°C	St Harmon (Powys)	3 Jul 1984
Scotland	-2.5°C	Lagganlia (Inverness-shire)	15 Jul 1977
Northern Ireland	-1.1°C	Lislap Forest (County Tyrone)	17 Jul 1971

Country	Pressure	Location	Date
Maximum pressure			
Scotland	1039.2 hPa	Aboyne (Aberdeenshire)	16 Jul 1996
Minimum pressure			
Scotland	967.9 hPa	Sule Skerry (Northern Isles)	8 Jul 1964

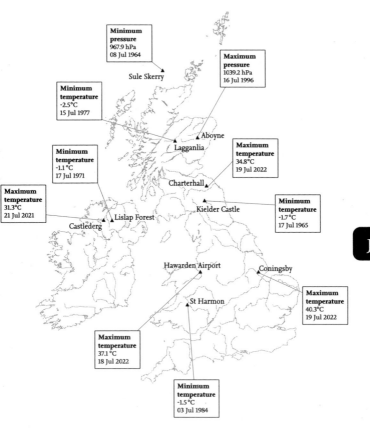

Minimum pressure
967.9 hPa
08 Jul 1964

Sule Skerry

Maximum pressure
1039.2 hPa
16 Jul 1996

Minimum temperature
-2.5°C
15 Jul 1977

Aboyne

Lagganlia

Maximum temperature
34.8°C
19 Jul 2022

Minimum temperature
-1.1°C
17 Jul 1971

Charterhall

Maximum temperature
31.3°C
21 Jul 2021

Kielder Castle

Minimum temperature
-1.7°C
17 Jul 1965

Castlederg

Lislap Forest

Hawarden Airport

Coningsby

Maximum temperature
40.3°C
19 Jul 2022

St Harmon

Maximum temperature
37.1°C
18 Jul 2022

Minimum temperature
-1.5°C
03 Jul 1984

J

The Weather in July 2023

Observation	Location	Date
Max. temperature 30.2°C	Chertsey, Abbey Mead (Surrey)	7 July
Min. temperature 1.2°C	Loch Glascarnoch (Ross & Cromarty)	26 July
Most rainfall 110.9 mm	White Barrow (Devon)	22 July
Most sunshine 16.1 hrs	Lerwick (Shetland)	8 July
Highest gust 79 mph (69 kt)	Needles Old Battery (Isle of Wight)	15 July

July was wetter and cooler than normal, with several summer storms. The jet stream was located further to the south and there was an abnormally large pressure gradient from the Azores High to the low over Scandinavia, resulting in autumnal weather. This being festival season, several events were adversely affected. On the 6th, the Tiree music festival was cancelled, and localised flooding made various other events washouts.

That weekend was the hottest of the month, with a high of 30.2°C recorded at Chertsey in Surrey. However, such high temperatures quickly broke down into thunderstorms. On the 8th, roads were flooded in Liverpool and north-east Wales, and there was surface flooding in Derbyshire and the West Midlands. Storms on the 9th were followed by more heavy rain over the next two days, resulting in disruption to rail services in central Scotland on the 10th and in Birmingham on the 11th.

Further disruption followed over the next two weeks as a series of fronts travelled west-to-east across the country. A particularly deep depression brought thunderstorms and high winds on the 15th; the south coast saw gusts touching

80 mph (129 kph/70 knots), while lightning caused a large-scale electricity outage in Northern Ireland on the 15th. Both Northern Ireland and Newcastle saw roads flooded and trees downed.

The following weekend saw another series of depressions bring the most persistent rain: 110.9 millimetres fell at White Barrow in Devon on the 22nd and the Garstang Flood Basin was opened to ease the pressure on local rivers. By the end of the month many drainage systems were at capacity, and even slightly unsettled weather saw localised flooding in Scarborough.

Overall, July was much more unsettled than June, with lower temperatures, higher winds and more rainfall. Daily maxima frequently failed to cross 20°C, and towards the end of the month minima fell, with 1.2°C recorded at Loch Glascarnoch. Lancashire, Merseyside, Manchester and parts of Northern Ireland recorded 200 per cent of their average rain. Overall, UK rainfall was 170 per cent of the average, making this the wettest July since 2009, while for Northern Ireland it was the wettest in 188 years. Sunshine was well below normal, with places in the south and west recording only 81 per cent of the normal.

Supercell

A supercell is an extremely violent, persistent thunderstorm that is marked by an extremely large, rotating updraught or 'mesocyclone'. Supercells are accompanied by heavy rain, large hail and frequent cloud-to-ground lightning discharges. The updraught may extend as high as 15 km into the atmosphere. The updraught is accompanied by strong downdraughts, but the two streams of air are separated horizontally in space, and this is one reason for a supercell's long lifetime (sometimes many hours) when compared with 'ordinary' thunderstorms, which may persist for about one hour. Cool downdraught air often bleeds into the mesocyclone and is the site of the formation of tornadoes.

Sunrise and Sunset 2025

Location	Date	Rise	Azimuth °	Set	Azimuth °
Belfast					
	1 Jul (Tue)	03:52	46	21:02	314
	11 Jul (Fri)	04:02	48	20:55	312
	21 Jul (Mon)	04:16	51	20:42	308
	31 Jul (Thu)	04:33	56	20:25	304
Cardiff					
	1 Jul (Tue)	04:00	50	20:32	310
	11 Jul (Fri)	04:09	52	20:26	308
	21 Jul (Mon)	04:21	55	20:16	305
	31 Jul (Thu)	04:35	59	20:01	301
Edinburgh					
	1 Jul (Tue)	03:31	44	21:01	316
	11 Jul (Fri)	03:42	46	20:53	314
	21 Jul (Mon)	03:57	50	20:39	310
	31 Jul (Thu)	04:15	55	20:21	305
London					
	1 Jul (Tue)	03:47	50	20:20	310
	11 Jul (Fri)	03:56	52	20:14	308
	21 Jul (Mon)	04:08	55	20:04	305
	31 Jul (Thu)	04:23	59	19:49	301

Note that all times are in Universal Time (UT), otherwise known as Greenwich Mean Time (GMT). These times do not take Summer Time (BST) into account.

Moonrise and Moonset 2025

Location	Date	Rise	Azimuth °	Set	Azimuth °
Belfast					
	1 Jul (Tue)	12:16	87	23:37	268
	11 Jul (Fri)	21:56	133	03:55	221
	21 Jul (Mon)	–	–	18:50	324
		23:51	40		
	31 Jul (Thu)	12:44	114	22:06	242
Cardiff					
	1 Jul (Tue)	11:06	87	23:27	268
	11 Jul (Fri)	21:26	130	04:07	226
	21 Jul (Mon)	00:04	44	18:11	319
	31 Jul (Thu)	12:24	112	22:06	244
Edinburgh					
	1 Jul (Tue)	11:04	87	23:26	268
	11 Jul (Fri)	21:54	135	03:32	219
	21 Jul (Mon)	–	–	18:53	327
		23:28	37		
	31 Jul (Thu)	12:37	115	21:50	241
London					
	1 Jul (Tue)	10:53	87	23:15	268
	11 Jul (Fri)	21:14	130	03:54	226
	21 Jul (Mon)	–	–	17:58	319
		23:51	44		
	31 Jul (Thu)	12:11	112	21:53	244

Note that all times are in Universal Time (UT), otherwise known as Greenwich Mean Time (GMT). These times do not take Summer Time (BST) into account.

Twilight Diagrams 2025

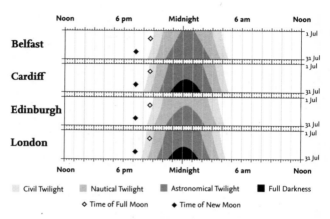

The exact times of the Moon's major phases are shown on the diagrams opposite.

Jet streams

Jet streams are narrow ribbons of fast-moving air, typically hundreds of kilometres wide and a few kilometres in depth. The most important one for British weather is the Polar Front Jet Stream, a westerly wind that flows right round the Earth. It is driven by the great temperature difference between the cold polar air and warmer air closer to the equator. Fluctuations in latitude are primarily caused by the flow across the Rockies in North America. These fluctuations in latitude, known as Rossby waves, spread right across the continental United States and across the Atlantic – and even farther. The jet stream has a great effect on the strength of depressions and also on their paths. It may cause depressions to sometimes pass directly across the British Isles and sometimes to the north or south of them.

The Moon's Phases and Ages 2025

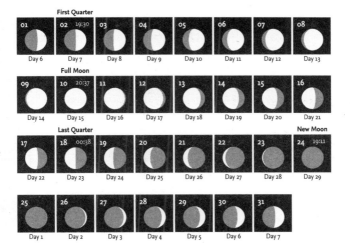

	First Quarter						
01	02 19:30	03	04	05	06	07	08
Day 6	Day 7	Day 8	Day 9	Day 10	Day 11	Day 12	Day 13
	Full Moon						
09	10 20:37	11	12	13	14	15	16
Day 14	Day 15	Day 16	Day 17	Day 18	Day 19	Day 20	Day 21
	Last Quarter						New Moon
17	18 00:38	19	20	21	22	23	24 19:11
Day 22	Day 23	Day 24	Day 25	Day 26	Day 27	Day 28	Day 29
25	26	27	28	29	30	31	
Day 1	Day 2	Day 3	Day 4	Day 5	Day 6	Day 7	

Gulf Stream

A warm-water current on the western side of the North Atlantic Ocean. It extends along the eastern seaboard of the United States from the Gulf of Mexico to Cape Hatteras. It then turns eastwards and becomes the North Atlantic Current. The warm water affecting the British Isles is a branch of this current, known as the North Atlantic Drift (often incorrectly called the Gulf Stream). This branch leaves the main current in the mid-Atlantic and, passing west of Ireland, heads up towards Norway and the Arctic Ocean.

July – In This Month

3 July 1996 – While rain interrupted play on Centre Court at Wimbledon, Cliff Richard was approached for an interview. He gave an impromptu concert for around 20 minutes until play was able to resume.

4 July 1915 – A hailstorm rated H6–7 struck areas from Highbridge in Somerset to Winslow in Buckinghamshire.

6 July 1988 – An explosion and subsequent oil and gas fires destroyed Piper Alpha oil platform, approximately 193 kilometres north-east of Aberdeen; 167 people were killed in the disaster.

10 July 1212 – The 'Great Fire of Southwark'. The flames were fanned by strong southerly winds, which pushed the fire towards the river, although it didn't cross London Bridge. Modern estimates place the number of fatalities at above 3,000.

13 July 1808 – A high of 37°C was recorded in Suffolk, part of a UK-wide heatwave that was the second hottest July on record at the time, and remains the ninth hottest on record.

24 July 1737 – Alexander Dalrymple, the first Hydrographer of the British Admiralty, was born. The UK Hydrographic Office remains a part of the Admiralty within the Ministry of Defence, and provides navigation, charting and marine management services around the world.

25–27 July 2007 – Flooding that had impacted the UK over the previous month reached its peak, with a fresh band of rain inundating the north and west of the UK. Sheffield received up to 70 millimetres of rain (more than the monthly average) in a matter of hours, and three deaths were recorded in Yorkshire and Lincolnshire. In Gloucestershire and Somerset the army was mobilised to provide fresh water to residents after water treatment works were flooded.

26 July 1540 – The German city of Einbeck was destroyed by fire, during a drought whose effects were felt across Europe. Only the summers of 2003 and (even more extreme) 2022 have matched the severity of that year.

J

The Drought of Summer 1976

Cracked earth, dried brown grass and parched reservoirs.
The summer of 1976 went down in history. As of early 2024, it
remains the sunniest summer on record, the second driest and
the fifth hottest. Temperatures topped 32.2°C for 15 consecutive
days between late June and early July. Water shortages caused
fields to dry up and standpipes were installed as one of the most
severe droughts on record approached its peak. However, the
wheels were set in motion long before the searing hot summer
of 1976.

The drought was the result of a very long dry period. Between
1971 and 1975, the total rainfall recorded was the lowest for any
five years since the 1850s. An exceptionally dry period then began
in May 1975. Both the summer and autumn of that year were very
dry and this theme continued through the winter. Rainy winter
months usually recharge groundwater levels, but a much drier

*The drought affected much of northern Europe, as shown by this dry
lake bed near Leersum in the Netherlands around the middle of the
month.*

The Grand Union Canal was closed to save water. Stockton Locks are pictured here on 23 July.

than average season meant that 1976 began on the back foot. By the end of winter, reservoirs in England and Wales were barely half full. Spring arrived, bringing little change in conditions, and as summer began, temperatures climbed in earnest. Temperatures reached their peak on 3 July 1976, hitting 35.9°C in Cheltenham, and on the very same day an emergency powers bill for water rationing was announced. Thousands of homes had their water supply turned off, to be replaced by standpipes installed in the streets. Families would have to collect water in buckets before carrying them home and emptying them into the bath. Farmers were unable to water their crops and thirsty livestock suffered in the sweltering conditions. In East Anglia, it became so dry that topsoil turned to dust and was blown away. Hot and dry weather persisted until the end of the summer. A Drought Act was introduced and a government Minister for Drought named. September rains finally brought an end to the 16-month drought, which was the driest period in 200 years. Due to its exceptional nature, the summer of '76 is often used in comparison whenever the weather takes a hot and dry turn. When the UK recorded its hottest temperature on record in July 2022, climate change deniers used the historical event to suggest that the hot weather was being exaggerated, as heatwaves have always happened. It is a dangerous statement to make. There is no doubt that the summer of 1976 was an exceptional period of weather. However, it was confined to the UK and Western Europe, while many other parts of the globe were cooler than average. In 2022, there were only a handful of places on Earth where temperatures were not considerably above average. The summer of 1976 was considered a once-in-500-years occurrence. But as the climate changes and hot weather becomes more frequent, heatwaves like that of 1976 are now 30 times more likely to occur.

August

Introduction

Although by all possible calendars, August is very much a summer month, it is typically the most unsettled month since March. Since they began naming storms in 2015, the UK Met Office have named four storms in August and even Professor Lamb's natural calendar refers to a 'late August stormy period'. High winds can be particularly damaging at this time of year as the trees are still in full leaf. This gives the tree more surface area and makes it more likely for branches to snap off and for trees to be uprooted.

The summer of 1912 saw the coldest, wettest and dullest August on record and was remembered in East Anglia for widespread flooding. The ground was already saturated before 186 millimetres of rain reportedly fell from 26–27 of August, around three to four times the amount of rain normally expected to fall in the month. The resultant floods destroyed or damaged the homes of 15,000 people.

Another destructive August storm that went down in history was the 1979 Fastnet Storm, also referred to as Low Y. It brought winds up to force 10 on the Beaufort scale, wreaking havoc on what was day three of the Fastnet race – a biennial yachting race in which the competitors sail from Cowes to Fastnet Rock (off the south-west coast of Ireland), then back to Plymouth (more recently Cherbourg) via the Scilly Isles. In total, 19 people lost their lives and around 4,000 people were involved in the rescue operation. Of the 303 yachts that started, only 86 finished the race, 24 were abandoned and 5 sank.

The race began on 11 August, at which time forecasts were predicting a ridge of high pressure to build and dominate conditions. However, a depression developed in the west Atlantic on 12 August and underwent explosive cyclogenesis (rapid deepening) as it moved towards the UK. Unfortunately, the area of strongest winds was out to sea, over the race.

It is still remembered as the deadliest yacht race in history, and resulted in a more cautious approach from the race directors in subsequent years. Twenty-eight years later in 2007, the start of the race was delayed following a forecast of extreme conditions. This meant that when the severe weather hit, the boats were in the relative safety of the English Channel, and 207 of the 271 boats taking part were able to retire safely.

History paints a rather bleak picture of August's weather conditions. Having said this, it is important to note that the month can also be calm, hot and sunny. Before the heatwaves of July 2019 and 2022 came along to take the lead, August used to hold the top spot for the hottest day on record. This was in Faversham, Kent in 2003, when temperatures reached 38.5°C.

A

Weather Extremes in August

Country	Temp.	Location	Date
Maximum temperature			
England	38.5°C	Faversham (Kent)	10 Aug 2003
Wales	35.2°C	Hawarden Bridge (Flintshire)	2 Aug 1990
Scotland	32.9°C	Greycrook (Scottish Borders)	9 Aug 2003
Northern Ireland	30.6°C	Tandragee Ballylisk (County Armagh)	2 Aug 1995
Minimum temperature			
England	-2.0°C	Kielder Castle (Northumberland)	14 Aug 1994
Wales	-2.8°C	Alwen (Conwy)	29 Aug 1959
Scotland	-4.5°C	Lagganlia (Inverness-shire)	21 Aug 1973
Northern Ireland	-1.9°C	Katesbridge (County Down)	24 Aug 2014

Country	Pressure	Location	Date
Maximum pressure			
Scotland	1038.4 hPa	Altnaharra No. 2 (Sutherland)	31 Aug 2021
Minimum pressure			
Republic of Ireland	967.3 hPa	Shannon Airport (County Clare)	19 Aug 2020

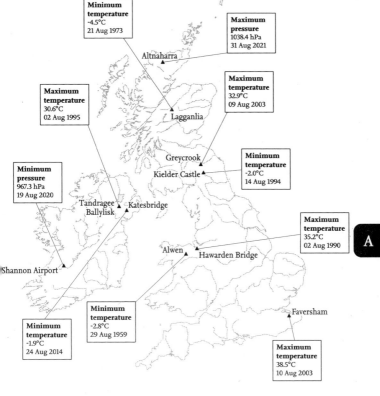

Minimum temperature
-4.5°C
21 Aug 1973

Maximum pressure
1038.4 hPa
31 Aug 2021

Altnaharra

Maximum temperature
32.9°C
09 Aug 2003

Maximum temperature
30.6°C
02 Aug 1995

Lagganlia

Greycrook

Minimum temperature
-2.0°C
14 Aug 1994

Kielder Castle

Minimum pressure
967.3 hPa
19 Aug 2020

Tandragee
Ballylisk
Katesbridge

Maximum temperature
35.2°C
02 Aug 1990

Alwen
Hawarden Bridge

A

Shannon Airport

Minimum temperature
-2.8°C
29 Aug 1959

Faversham

Minimum temperature
-1.9°C
24 Aug 2014

Maximum temperature
38.5°C
10 Aug 2003

133

The Weather in August 2023

Observation	Location	Date
Max. temperature 28.4°C	Wellesbourne (Warwickshire)	10 August
Min. temperature 1.4°C	Altnaharra No. 2 (Sutherland)	6 August
Most rainfall 83.0 mm	Trassey Slievenaman (County Down)	18 August
Most sunshine 14.7 hrs	Stornoway Airport (Western Isles)	1 August
Highest gust 78 mph (125 kph/65 kt)	Berry Head (Devon)	5 August

August continued the unsettled pattern of July, with the Azores High struggling to extend its normal influence over the UK and a series of Atlantic depressions arriving instead, although low pressure dominated to a lesser extent than in the previous month. The south and east saw the majority of the warm weather, and there were several cool spells during which temperatures struggled to breach 15°C.

The month also saw two unseasonal named storms: Storm Antoni arrived on the 5th, with amber wind warnings issued, and 70 mph (113 kph/61 knots) gusts saw transport and holiday events disrupted in Wales and south-west England. Power cuts affected 1,500 properties in Cornwall. Later in the month, Storm Betty brought more wind and heavy rain on the 18th and 19th, although the impacts were less severe. A third significant low-pressure system swept across northern England and south-east Scotland from the 25th to 27th. Although not marked enough to warrant a name, much of Merseyside and north Cheshire were affected by flooding, and two people died when a car was submerged underneath a railway bridge.

The main exception to this pattern was on the 8th to 10th when higher pressure prevailed and a south-easterly airstream was established. On the 10th, large parts of the country recorded temperatures in the mid to high twenties, including a monthly high of 28.4°C at Wellesbourne in Warwickshire.

Temperatures and rainfall were all near average overall. Minimum temperatures were slightly above average in northern and western areas, while the UK monthly mean temperature was 0.2°C above average. Rainfall was 95 per cent of average and sunshine was at 92 per cent. However, this hides a much more variable story across different areas and through the month. For instance, Wales saw only 79 per cent of its average sunshine and, while parts of the midlands and western Scotland saw less than 50 per cent of average rainfall, Trassey Slievenaman in County Down received over half its monthly average in the space of 12 hours on the night of the 18th–19th.

This was the second time since the introduction of the naming system in 2015 that the UK saw two named storms in August (the other being 2020). With global climate change causing increasing variation to normal weather patterns, it may well not be the last.

Ionosphere
A region of the atmosphere, consisting of the upper mesosphere and part of the exosphere (from about 60–70 km to 1,000 km or more) where radiation from the Sun ionises atoms and causes high electrical conductivity. The ionosphere both reflects certain radio waves back towards the surface, and blocks some wavelengths of radiation from space.

A

Sunrise and Sunset 2025

Location	Date	Rise	Azimuth °	Set	Azimuth °
Belfast					
	1 Aug (Fri)	04:34	56	20:24	303
	11 Aug (Mon)	04:52	62	20:03	298
	21 Aug (Thu)	05:10	68	19:41	292
	31 Aug (Sun)	05:29	74	19:17	286
Cardiff					
	1 Aug (Fri)	04:36	59	20:00	301
	11 Aug (Mon)	04:52	64	19:42	296
	21 Aug (Thu)	05:08	69	19:22	290
	31 Aug (Sun)	05:24	75	19:00	285
Edinburgh					
	1 Aug (Fri)	04:17	55	20:19	305
	11 Aug (Mon)	04:36	61	19:58	299
	21 Aug (Thu)	04:56	67	19:34	293
	31 Aug (Sun)	05:15	73	19:09	286
London					
	1 Aug (Fri)	04:24	59	19:48	301
	11 Aug (Mon)	04:39	64	19:30	296
	21 Aug (Thu)	04:55	69	19:10	290
	31 Aug (Sun)	05:11	75	18:48	285

Note that all times are in Universal Time (UT), otherwise known as Greenwich Mean Time (GMT). These times do not take Summer Time (BST) into account.

Moonrise and Moonset 2025

Location	Date	Rise	Azimuth °	Set	Azimuth °
Belfast					
	1 Aug (Fri)	14:02	124	22:17	233
	11 Aug (Mon)	20:48	95	07:27	258
	21 Aug (Thu)	02:14	47	19:26	307
	31 Aug (Sun)	15:35	143	21:23	216
Cardiff					
	1 Aug (Fri)	13:36	121	22:20	229
	11 Aug (Mon)	20:35	95	07:20	259
	21 Aug (Thu)	02:22	50	19:00	304
	31 Aug (Sun)	14:57	138	21:39	221
Edinburgh					
	1 Aug (Fri)	13:57	125	21:58	232
	11 Aug (Mon)	20:38	95	07:13	258
	21 Aug (Thu)	01:53	45	19:22	308
	31 Aug (Sun)	15:37	146	20:58	213
London					
	1 Aug (Fri)	13:24	121	22:08	236
	11 Aug (Mon)	20:23	95	07:07	259
	21 Aug (Thu)	02:09	50	18:48	304
	31 Aug (Sun)	14:44	138	21:26	221

A

Note that all times are in Universal Time (UT), otherwise known as Greenwich Mean Time (GMT). These times do not take Summer Time (BST) into account.

Twilight Diagrams 2025

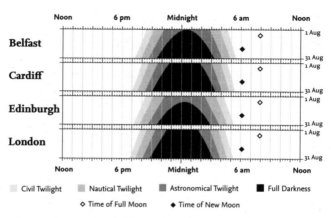

| Civil Twilight | Nautical Twilight | Astronomical Twilight | Full Darkness |
| ◇ Time of Full Moon | ◆ Time of New Moon |

The exact times of the Moon's major phases are shown on the diagrams opposite.

Föhn effect

When humid air is forced to rise over high ground, it normally deposits some precipitation in the form of rain or snow. When the air descends on the far side of the hills, because it has lost some of its moisture, it warms at a greater rate than it cooled on its ascent. This 'föhn effect' may cause temperatures on the leeward side of hills or mountains to be much warmer than locations at a corresponding altitude on the windward side.

The Moon's Phases and Ages 2025

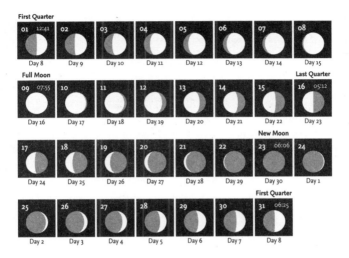

First Quarter

01 12:41	02	03	04	05	06	07	08
Day 8	Day 9	Day 10	Day 11	Day 12	Day 13	Day 14	Day 15

Full Moon / **Last Quarter**

09 07:55	10	11	12	13	14	15	16 05:12
Day 16	Day 17	Day 18	Day 19	Day 20	Day 21	Day 22	Day 23

New Moon

17	18	19	20	21	22	23 06:06	24
Day 24	Day 25	Day 26	Day 27	Day 28	Day 29	Day 30	Day 1

First Quarter

25	26	27	28	29	30	31 06:25
Day 2	Day 3	Day 4	Day 5	Day 6	Day 7	Day 8

Advection
The horizontal motion of air from one area to another. Advection of humid air over cold ground will often result in the ground cooling the overlying air, and is a common cause of mist and fog. Advection also brings sea mist onto low-lying coastal areas.

A

August – In This Month

1–12 August 1938 – A series of thunderstorms arrived over England and Wales; one of the longest periods of successive summer days of stormy weather in the UK.

2 August 1908 – Two people died in a tornado in Guildford, on a day of intense storms across the south of England.

3 August 1912 – Frost was reported in Aberdeen, marking the low point of the wettest, coldest and dullest August of the twentieth century. The average rainfall across the UK was 183 millimetres, or 231 per cent of the expected amount, and on the 26th this led to the Great Norfolk Flood.

3 August 1990 – A temperature of 37.1°C was reached in Cheltenham, Gloucestershire, the hottest recorded in the twentieth century.

15 August 1858 – The first transatlantic telegraph communication was achieved. Over the next few years multiple transatlantic telegraph cables were laid, with companies advertising the new communication speeds as 'two weeks in two minutes'.

16 August 2004 – The Boscastle flood occurred in two Cornish villages. This was a flash flood after eight hours of exceptional rain, with the peak flow of the flood waters measured at 140 cubic metres per second.

18 August 1932 – The second heatwave in a month hit the UK as low pressure brought hot air north from the Mediterranean, with 35°C recorded at Jersey, and 36.1°C in London the following day. In France, temperatures rose above 40°C before thunderstorms on the 20th and 21st brought them back down again.

29 August 1956 – There were severe floods in the Scottish Borders and East Lothian. The River Tweed overtopped its banks at Peebles, and at Haddington boats had to be sent from North Berwick to help people escape the flooding.

A

Hornsea 2

In August 2022, the world's largest offshore wind farm became operational. Located 88 kilometres off the coast of Yorkshire, Hornsea 2 provides power to more than 1.4 million homes in the UK. Comprised of 165 wind turbines, Hornsea 2 covers an area of 462 square kilometres in the southern North Sea. It is an ideal location for offshore wind farms because of its proximity to land and shallow water depth.

However, the variable weather of the UK does not make construction of such large and ambitious projects very easy. A range of different weather conditions come into play, each presenting different challenges. Although strong winds are desirable for power generation, they tend to complicate the construction phases of wind farms, often bringing rough seas and halting progress, as the vessels used to transport workers offshore can only deposit their cargo when waves are below a certain height. Lightning and fog also present an issue. Lightning is most frequent in the south and east of the UK, while strong winds and high waves are more likely in waters to the north and west, meaning that wherever a wind farm is built it will face some means of weather disruption.

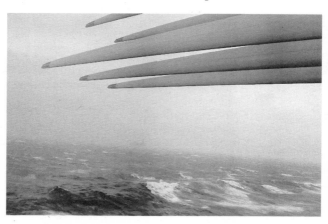

Challenging weather conditions during the construction of Hornsea 2.

Onshore construction faces another set of issues. Cables must be installed to connect each wind farm to the National Grid, and whether underground or over, it can be a controversial issue with nearby residents. As more and more renewable energy projects are built, further strain is placed on existing infrastructure. To address this, the National Grid are planning a series of projects, known as The Great Grid Update, which is claimed to be the largest overhaul of the electricity network in generations. For Hornsea 2, a total of 350,000 metres of cable was installed across 39 kilometres of Lincolnshire countryside back in 2020 and early 2021.

Hornsea 2 is unlikely to hold its title of the 'world's largest offshore wind farm' for long. To the north of the Hornsea wind farms lies Dogger Bank. This isolated sand bank, which once connected the UK to mainland Europe and was known as 'Doggerland', will be home to the Dogger Bank Wind Farm. With water depths of only 18–63 metres, its shallow nature provides the perfect home for an offshore wind farm. Construction is currently underway, and the new wind farm is expected to be fully operational in 2026.

The completed Hornsea 2 wind farm pictured at sunset.

A

September

Introduction

While, for much of the population, early September means the end of the summer holidays and back to school, for meteorologists, the first day of September brings the beginning of autumn. However, defining autumn as one of five natural seasons brings a slightly later start – 10 September to 19 November, and if you're an astronomer, autumn won't begin until the equinox on 22 September (2025).

September also hails the start of a new storm season. The Met Office began naming storms in 2015, hoping to promote clear communication across meteorological, media and government organisations, as well as raising awareness of potential impacts to the public. Currently, the naming system is a collaboration between the UK Met Office, Ireland's Met Éireann and KNMI, the Dutch meteorological service. Rather than meeting set criteria, storms are named more subjectively, depending on potential impacts and their likelihood.

Despite beginning in September, the storm season does not typically reach its height until later in the autumn and winter. Instead, September is often a settled month. It is generally drier than the two months either side and is the second period of the year in which the weather is most likely to be dominated by anticyclonic conditions, following April–May. Should high pressure develop, fine weather can persist for much of the month and westerly dominated conditions are unlikely to return until October. Although days are beginning to shorten in earnest and daylight hours reducing, September can bring warm, and even hot weather. This is often helped by the seas surrounding Britain and Ireland, which due to seasonal lag are still fairly warm.

However, with the nights drawing in, temperatures begin to fall lower overnight. Ground and other surfaces often cool faster than air, and if this is the case, water droplets in the air can condense onto these surfaces, forming dew. The temperature at which these droplets form is known as the dew point.

If you wake to a covering of droplets on your lawn and some bright autumn sunshine, you may be lucky enough to catch a glimpse of a rare weather phenomenon – a dewbow. Similar to a rainbow, which is formed when raindrops scatter rays of sunlight, a dewbow is formed by the refraction of light from drops of dew. If you want to spot one, you'll need to stand with your back to the Sun and look down at the ground on a cold, dewy autumn morning. They can also form on cobwebs, colouring them in spectacular rainbow hues.

However, dewbows aren't the only exciting spectacle to look out for this month. On the evening of 7 September 2025, providing skies aren't too cloudy, you may be able to catch a total lunar eclipse. At this point, expected to be around 7:30 p.m. BST, the Moon will appear red as it is not illuminated directly by the Sun, but by light which has been refracted through the Earth's atmosphere.

Stratosphere

The second layer in the atmosphere, lying above the troposphere, in which temperatures either stabilise or begin to increase with height. This increase of temperature is primarily driven by the absorption of solar energy by ozone in the ozone layer. In the lowermost region, between the tropopause and about a height of 20 kilometres, the temperature is stable. Above that there is an overall increase to the top of the stratosphere (the stratopause) at an altitude of about 50 kilometres.

S

Weather Extremes in September

Country	Temp.	Location	Date
Maximum temperature			
England	35.6°C	Bawtry, Hesley Hall (South Yorkshire)	2 Sep 1906
Wales	32.3°C	Hawarden Bridge (Flintshire)	1 Sep 1906
Scotland	32.2°C	Gordon Castle (Moray)	1 Sep 1906
Northern Ireland	28.0°C	Castlederg (County Tyrone)	8 Sep 2023
Minimum temperature			
England	-5.6°C	Santon Downham (Norfolk) Grendon Underwood (Buckinghamshire)	30 Sep 1969
Wales	-5.5°C	St Harmon (Powys)	19 Sep 1986
Scotland	-6.7°C	Dalwhinnie (Highland)	26 Sep 1942
Northern Ireland	-3.7°C	Katesbridge (County Down)	27 Sep 2020

Country	Pressure	Location	Date
Maximum pressure			
Northern Ireland	1042.0 hPa	Ballykelly (County Londonderry)	11 Sep 2009
Minimum pressure			
Republic of Ireland	957.1 hPa	Claremorris (County Mayo)	21 Sep 1953

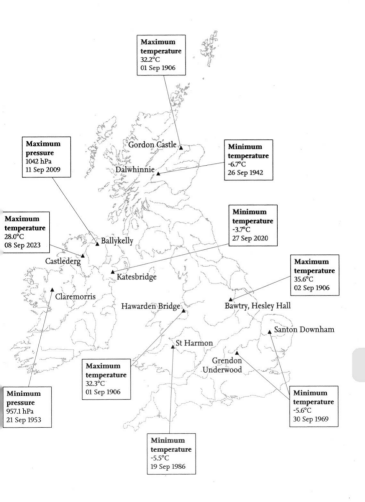

Maximum temperature
32.2°C
01 Sep 1906

Maximum pressure
1042 hPa
11 Sep 2009

Minimum temperature
-6.7°C
26 Sep 1942

Gordon Castle

Dalwhinnie

Maximum temperature
28.0°C
08 Sep 2023

Minimum temperature
-3.7°C
27 Sep 2020

Ballykelly

Castlederg

Katesbridge

Maximum temperature
35.6°C
02 Sep 1906

Claremorris

Hawarden Bridge

Bawtry, Hesley Hall

Santon Downham

St Harmon

Grendon Underwood

Minimum pressure
957.1 hPa
21 Sep 1953

Maximum temperature
32.3°C
01 Sep 1906

Minimum temperature
-5.6°C
30 Sep 1969

Minimum temperature
-5.5°C
19 Sep 1986

The Weather in September 2023

Observation	Location	Date
Max. temperature 33.5°C	Faversham (Kent)	10 September
Min. temperature -3.5°C	Kinbrace, Hatchery (Sutherland)	13 September
Most rainfall 117.0 mm	Honister Pass (Cumbria)	19 September
Most sunshine 12.9 hrs	Oxford Brampton No. 3 (Cumbria)	4 September 5 September
Highest gust 84 mph (135 kph/73 kt)	Capel Curig No. 3 (Gwynedd)	27 September

In stark contrast to August, the first half of September saw high pressure dominate, with much of the UK seeing its most significant warm period since June. A heatwave from the 4th to the 10th saw temperatures exceed 30°C somewhere in the country for seven consecutive days. The hottest day of the year was recorded on the 10th, with 33.5°C at Faversham in Kent, only the fifth time on record that the year's maximum temperature was reached in September. This period also saw a new September temperature record set for Northern Ireland: 28.0°C, recorded at Castlederg on the 8th.

On the 10th, as the heatwave broke down, thunderstorms and intense downpours caused flash flooding, with rainfall rates exceeding 30 millimetres per hour and the Cumbrian hills receiving more than 60 millimetres over 24 hours. Transport disruption left thousands of runners taking part in the Great North Run stranded after the event. This precipitated a much more unsettled second half of the month, with westerly winds bringing more traditional autumnal rain and some places in the north of Scotland recording their first frosts of the season. Rain on the 19th and 20th caused flooding in North Wales, and disrupted transport in the South Pennine and Inverclyde areas.

Particularly notable was Storm Agnes, the first named storm of the 2023–24 winter storm season, which arrived on the 27th. It brought strong winds and flooding; a woman had to be rescued from her car in Northern Ireland after it became stranded in a flood, and the Met Office issued danger to life warnings due to flying debris and falling trees. However, the storm had in fact weakened considerably by the time it made landfall in the UK and, while some power outages were reported, the effects were less severe than they might have been.

Overall, temperatures were higher than expected, with maximum temperatures as much as 4°C above the long-term average in parts of the south-east. The UK's monthly mean temperature was 2.2°C above average at 15.2°C, making this the equal warmest September on record (joint with 2006). Sunshine totals were slightly above average at 112 per cent across the UK. However, rainfall was also above average, at 131 per cent. Much of this fell as thundery downpours, leading to an uneven distribution across the UK; Exeter Airport had to close due to flooding on the 17th and 18th, while parts of Essex and Kent received less than 50 per cent of their average rainfall.

S

Sunrise and Sunset 2025

Location	Date	Rise	Azimuth °	Set	Azimuth °
Belfast					
	1 Sep (Mon)	05:31	75	19:14	285
	11 Sep (Thu)	05:49	81	18:49	279
	21 Sep (Sun)	06:07	88	18:24	272
	30 Sep (Tue)	06:24	94	18:01	266
Cardiff					
	1 Sep (Mon)	05:25	76	18:58	284
	11 Sep (Thu)	05:41	82	18:35	278
	21 Sep (Sun)	05:57	88	18:12	272
	30 Sep (Tue)	06:12	94	17:52	266
Edinburgh					
	1 Sep (Mon)	05:17	74	19:06	286
	11 Sep (Thu)	05:36	81	18:40	279
	21 Sep (Sun)	05:56	88	18:13	272
	30 Sep (Tue)	06:14	94	17:50	266
London					
	1 Sep (Mon)	05:13	76	18:46	284
	11 Sep (Thu)	05:29	82	18:23	278
	21 Sep (Sun)	05:45	88	18:00	272
	30 Sep (Tue)	05:59	94	17:40	266

Note that all times are in Universal Time (UT), otherwise known as Greenwich Mean Time (GMT). These times do not take Summer Time (BST) into account.

Moonrise and Moonset 2025

Location	Date	Rise	Azimuth °	Set	Azimuth °
Belfast					
	1 Sep (Mon)	16:39	146	22:08	214
	11 Sep (Thu)	19:37	53	11:13	303
	21 Sep (Sun)	05:34	85	18:10	270
	30 Sep (Tue)	16:00	142	22:06	219
Cardiff					
	1 Sep (Mon)	15:59	140	22:25	220
	11 Sep (Thu)	19:40	56	10:48	317
	21 Sep (Sun)	05:25	85	17:59	270
	30 Sep (Tue)	15:24	138	22:19	224
Edinburgh					
	1 Sep (Mon)	16:43	149	22:41	211
	11 Sep (Thu)	19:18	52	11:08	304
	21 Sep (Sun)	05:22	85	17:59	270
	30 Sep (Tue)	16:02	145	21:41	216
London					
	1 Sep (Mon)	15:47	140	22:12	219
	11 Sep (Thu)	19:28	56	10:35	300
	21 Sep (Sun)	05:12	85	17:47	270
	30 Sep (Tue)	15:11	138	22:06	224

S

Note that all times are in Universal Time (UT), otherwise known as Greenwich Mean Time (GMT). These times do not take Summer Time (BST) into account.

Twilight Diagrams 2025

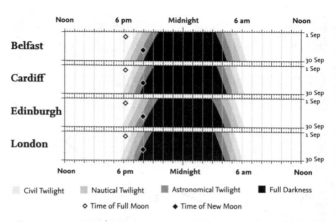

| Civil Twilight | Nautical Twilight | Astronomical Twilight | Full Darkness |

◇ Time of Full Moon   ◆ Time of New Moon

The exact times of the Moon's major phases are shown on the diagrams opposite.

Mesosphere

The third layer of the atmosphere, above the stratosphere and below the thermosphere. It extends from about 50 km (the height of the stratopause) to about 86–100 km (the mesopause). Within it, temperature decreases with increasing altitude, reaching the atmospheric minimum of approximately -123°C at the mesopause. The only clouds occurring within the mesosphere are noctilucent clouds.

The Moon's Phases and Ages 2025

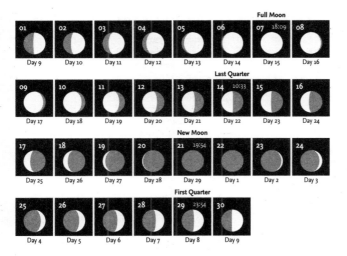

Full Moon

01	02	03	04	05	06	07 18:09	08
Day 9	Day 10	Day 11	Day 12	Day 13	Day 14	Day 15	Day 16

Last Quarter

09	10	11	12	13	14 10:33	15	16
Day 17	Day 18	Day 19	Day 20	Day 21	Day 22	Day 23	Day 24

New Moon

17	18	19	20	21 19:54	22	23	24
Day 25	Day 26	Day 27	Day 28	Day 29	Day 1	Day 2	Day 3

First Quarter

25	26	27	28	29 23:54	30
Day 4	Day 5	Day 6	Day 7	Day 8	Day 9

Thermosphere
The fourth layer of the atmosphere, counting from the surface.
It is tenuous and lies above the upper limit of the mesosphere,
the mesopause, at approximately 86–100 km, and extends
into interplanetary space. Within it, the temperature increases
continuously with height.

S

September – In This Month

5 September 1885 – *Scientific American* published the 'first' photograph of lightning, taken by William Jennings in 1882. However, he may have been beaten to it by Thomas Martin Easterly in 1847, who captured a lightning strike using a daguerreotype (though this technique results in a less clear image than Jennings captured).

6 September 1776 – John Dalton was born. At the age of 21 he began a meteorological diary that he kept for 57 years, recording over 200,000 observations.

6 September 2008 – The River Wansbeck burst its banks following heavy rainfall over the previous 24 hours, overwhelming Morpeth's flood defences and damaging nearly 1,000 properties.

15 September 1968 – The worst day of the Great Flood saw train passengers stranded, and a French cyclist was killed when an electricity cable fell into a flooded road. Across the Home Counties, more than 14,000 homes were flooded.

15 September 2000 – A pumping station at Eastney failed after 58 millimetres of rain fell in 4 $^1/_2$ hours, causing flooding in Portsmouth. This marked the start of three months of severe flooding, as several extratropical cyclones brough record rain to the UK. The jet stream was displaced to the south of average, resulting in a near-stationary front along which this succession of low-pressure systems moved throughout September, October and November.

22 September 1935 – An H6 level hailstorm tracked from Newport in Monmouthshire to Mundesley in Norfolk, the longest continuous hail swath on record in Britain.

24 September 2019 – Localised flash flooding was reported across England, with roads and railways disrupted in the north-west, south-east and the Midlands.

S

William Jennings's photograh of lightning taken in 1882 and published in
Scientific American.

Thomas Martin Easterly's 1847 daguerrotype of a streak of lightning.

The Carrington Event

Without the Sun, complex life on Earth would cease to exist. Its gravity holds the solar system together and its light provides a source of heat. Although from Earth it seems like a distant, unchanging ball of light, the Sun is incredibly active. It is constantly emitting a stream of electrically charged particles, known as solar wind. This can be disrupted by eruptions of plasma, known as coronal mass ejections (CMEs), or bursts of light and charged particles, called solar flares. Both can affect the solar wind, creating geomagnetic storms.

On 1 September 1859, the largest geomagnetic storm on record took out telegraph communications and disrupted power grids around the world. It was named the Carrington Event, after the British astronomer, Richard Carrington, who had observed the solar flare through his telescope. As well as communications chaos, it brought spectacular displays of aurora borealis as particles from the Sun interacted with Earth's atmosphere. While they are normally confined to the Arctic Circle, during the Carrington Event, the Northern Lights were visible as far south as the Caribbean and Hawaii.

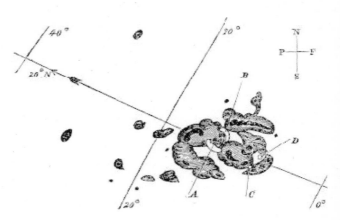

Carrington's drawing of the solar flare in 1859.

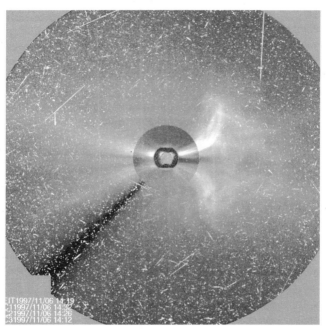

A composite image of a coronal mass ejection as seen from NASA's SOHO satellite on 6 November 1997. The sun and ejected matter are at the centre, and the white streaks of light around these are from protons hitting the satellite, showing the 'snowy' interference typical of the effect of CMEs on digital communications equipment.

The Carrington Event occurred during a solar maximum, which is a period of increased activity from the Sun. During this time, CMEs, solar flares and sunspots are more likely. At solar minimum, the activity is much lower. These phases of high and low activity make up the solar cycle, which lasts around 11 years. The latest solar cycle began in December 2019, declared by a group of scientists when the solar minimum had occurred. Since then, activity has been gradually increasing and is expected to continue until the next predicted solar maximum around 2024–25, but we won't know when the maximum occurred until we're far beyond it.

The Carrington Event took place before the invention of digital technology but since then, smaller geomagnetic storms have also caused regionalised power outages and surges, disruption to satellites and radio communications. Given our increasing reliance on digital communication and the potential disruptions that the Sun can bring, there is a lot of pressure on scientists to predict geomagnetic storms. In 2014, the Met Office launched the Met Office Space Weather Operations Center, partnering with similar organisations across the world, with the aim of forecasting severe space weather events and mitigating the impacts.

October

Introduction

With autumn well and truly underway, October often brings the turning of the leaves. As days continue to shorten, trees begin to close down their food production systems and produce less chlorophyll – the chemical that makes leaves green. With chlorophyll reducing, other chemicals become more prevalent, green giving way to a vibrant array of colours, from pale yellow to deepest purple.

Depending on the strength of the winds in this month, leaves also begin to fall. Although widely considered to be a North American word for autumn, 'fall' was commonly used in England until relatively recently, as a shortened version of 'fall of the leaf' – a common phrase in the seventeenth century. In the eighteenth century, it was replaced with autumn, derived from the French 'automne', of uncertain meaning.

Meteorologically speaking, October's weather is varied and changeable. As the jet stream reinvigorates, the number of Atlantic depressions sweeping across the country increases. Strong winds and rain are likely during this month, with moist and mild maritime air bringing frequent downpours and cloudy skies, occasionally punctuated by brighter, more showery days following the clearance of a cold front.

Temperatures continue to drop, leading to the first frosts of the season. These can be extensive, but perhaps not quite reaching the far south of the country. Snow may even be possible if winds turn to the north and cold air advances from the Arctic, which is cooling rapidly as winter approaches.

However, periods of warm, anticyclonic weather are still possible. The highest October temperature on record was set in Kent in 2011, when the mercury soared to 29.9°C at the very beginning of the month. High pressure centred over continental Europe, combined with a low-pressure system to the south of Iceland, led to a southerly flow becoming established across the UK in the days leading up to the record-breaking warmth.

When these unseasonably warm spells of weather occur, you'll often hear the phrase 'Indian summer' thrown around. It is unclear where this phrase comes from and with either South Asian or Native American origins carrying heavy colonial connotations, many meteorological organisations choose not to use it.

Before this term became widely used in the nineteenth century, periods of autumnal warmth were named after Christian saints whose feast days fall around this time. 'St Luke's Little Summer' was used to describe a spell of warm weather around 18 October, while 'St Martin's Summer' was used if the warm spell was later in November.

O

Weather Extremes in October

Country	Temp.	Location	Date
Maximum temperature			
England	29.9°C	Gravesend (Kent)	1 Oct 2011
Wales	28.2°C	Hawarden Airport (Flintshire)	1 Oct 2011
Scotland	27.4°C	Tillypronie (Aberdeenshire)	3 Oct 1908
Northern Ireland	24.1°C	Strabane (County Tyrone)	10 Oct 1969
Minimum temperature			
England	-10.6°C	Wark (Northumberland)	17 Oct 1993
Wales	-9.4°C	Rhayader, Penvalley (Pows)	26 Oct 1931
Scotland	-11.7°C	Dalwhinnie (Highland)	28 Oct 1948
Northern Ireland	-7.2°C	Lough Navar Forest (County Fermanagh)	18 Oct 1993

Country	Pressure	Location	Date
Maximum pressure			
Scotland	1045.6 hPa	Dyce (Aberdeenshire)	31 Oct 1956
Minimum pressure			
Scotland	946.8 hPa	Cawdor Castle (Nairnshire)	14 Oct 1891

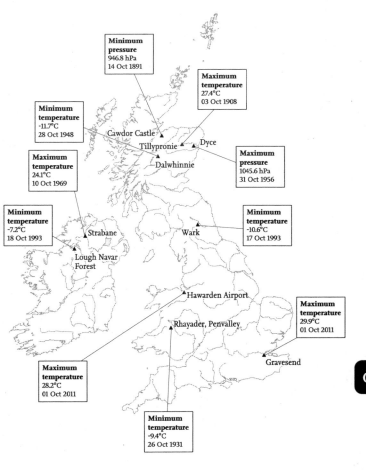

Minimum pressure
946.8 hPa
14 Oct 1891

Maximum temperature
27.4°C
03 Oct 1908

Minimum temperature
-11.7°C
28 Oct 1948

Cawdor Castle

Tillypronie — Dyce

Maximum pressure
1045.6 hPa
31 Oct 1956

Dalwhinnie

Maximum temperature
24.1°C
10 Oct 1969

Minimum temperature
-7.2°C
18 Oct 1993

Strabane

Wark

Minimum temperature
-10.6°C
17 Oct 1993

Lough Navar Forest

Hawarden Airport

Rhayader, Penvalley

Maximum temperature
29.9°C
01 Oct 2011

Gravesend

Maximum temperature
28.2°C
01 Oct 2011

Minimum temperature
-9.4°C
26 Oct 1931

O

The Weather in October 2023

Observation	Location	Date
Max. temperature 26.1°C	East Malling (Kent)	9 October
Min. temperature -5.5°C	Dalwhinnie No. 2 (Inverness-shire)	31 October
Most rainfall 129.5 mm	Fettercairn, Glensaugh No. 2 (Kincardineshire)	19 October
Most sunshine 10.1 hrs	Exeter Airport (Devon)	8 October
Highest gust 86 mph (138 kph/96 kt)	Needles Old Battery (Isle of Wight)	29 October

The first half of October from the 1st to the 13th saw a series of depressions from the Atlantic cross the UK, which brought high rainfall. Mickleden Middlefell Farm in Cumbria received 124.6 millimetres on the 5th, while an 'atmospheric river' event saw Scotland receive an average of 64.1 millimetres on the 6th and 7th, its wettest two-day period on record. This caused several road and rail closures, and significant flood damage to crops. In between these depressions, high pressure over western Europe caused spikes in temperature over southern areas, particularly between the 7th and 10th, when temperatures in England and Wales reached more than 8°C above average for the time of year. Further north and in Scotland, the weather was more consistently wet.

Later in the month, higher pressure over the UK led to clear but cold weather, with frosts widely reported and temperatures in northern England and southern Scotland dipping to almost -5°C between the 14th and 17th. Total rainfall over these few days was almost none, while maximum temperatures struggled to reach above 10°C in many places.

On the 18th, the second named storm of the autumn arrived. Storm Babet brought persistent red warnings for rain and strong winds to northern England and eastern Scotland, and remained over these areas for a number of days due to a blocking high over Scandinavia. Some places received over a month's average rainfall in less than 48 hours, causing over 30,000 homes in northern Scotland to lose power and at least seven people to lose their lives. Leeds Bradford Airport was closed after an aircraft skidded off the runway, and 45 workers had to be airlifted off a North Sea oil platform after it lost anchors. Continuing rain over the following days meant some areas of central Scotland remained flooded at the end of the month, and Angus Council estimated the flood damage would cost in excess of £4 million to repair.

Overall, the month was predominantly mild and wet, driven by the presence of a low-pressure anomaly to the south-west of Ireland for much of it. Many areas set new monthly rainfall records, and parts of eastern Scotland, Northern Ireland and eastern and northern England saw well over twice the average October rainfall. Temperatures were slightly above average, particularly in southern England and Wales.

***

Typhoon
The term used for a tropical cyclone in the western Pacific Ocean. Typhoons are some of the strongest systems encountered anywhere on Earth.

O

Sunrise and Sunset 2025

Location	Date	Rise	Azimuth °	Set	Azimuth °
Belfast					
	1 Oct (Wed)	06:26	95	17:59	265
	11 Oct (Sat)	06:45	101	17:34	259
	21 Oct (Tue)	07:04	108	17:11	252
	31 Oct (Fri)	07:24	114	16:49	246
Cardiff					
	1 Oct (Wed)	06:13	94	17:50	265
	11 Oct (Sat)	06:30	101	17:27	259
	21 Oct (Tue)	06:47	106	17:08	253
	31 Oct (Fri)	07:04	112	16:47	248
Edinburgh					
	1 Oct (Wed)	06:16	95	17:47	265
	11 Oct (Sat)	06:36	102	17:21	258
	21 Oct (Tue)	06:56	108	16:57	251
	31 Oct (Fri)	07:17	115	16:34	245
London					
	1 Oct (Wed)	06:01	94	17:37	265
	11 Oct (Sat)	06:18	100	17:15	259
	21 Oct (Tue)	06:35	106	16:54	253
	31 Oct (Fri)	06:52	112	16:34	248

Note that all times are in Universal Time (UT), otherwise known as Greenwich Mean Time (GMT). These times do not take Summer Time (BST) into account.

Moonrise and Moonset 2025

Location	Date	Rise	Azimuth °	Set	Azimuth °
Belfast					
	1 Oct (Wed)	16:26	136	23:29	226
	11 Oct (Sat)	19:13	35	13:30	324
	21 Oct (Tue)	08:10	113	16:41	243
	31 Oct (Fri)	15:11	111	–	–
				01:24	253
Cardiff					
	1 Oct (Wed)	15:54	132	23:36	230
	11 Oct (Sat)	19:30	40	12:51	319
	21 Oct (Tue)	06:50	111	16:40	245
	31 Oct (Fri)	14:52	110	–	–
				01:19	254
Edinburgh					
	1 Oct (Wed)	16:25	138	23:07	224
	11 Oct (Sat)	18:47	32	13:33	327
	21 Oct (Tue)	07:03	114	16:26	243
	31 Oct (Fri)	15:04	112	–	–
				01:10	253
London					
	1 Oct (Wed)	15:42	132	23:23	230
	11 Oct (Sat)	19:17	40	12:38	319
	21 Oct (Tue)	06:37	111	16:28	246
	31 Oct (Fri)	14:40	110	–	–
				01:06	254

O

Note that all times are in Universal Time (UT), otherwise known as Greenwich Mean Time (GMT). These times do not take Summer Time (BST) into account.

Twilight Diagrams 2025

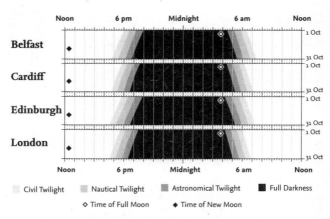

The exact times of the Moon's major phases are shown on the diagrams opposite.

Icelandic Low

A semi-permanent feature of the distribution of pressure over the North Atlantic. Unlike the more-or-less permanent Azores High, it largely arises because depressions (low-pressure systems) frequently pass across the area. A similar low-pressure area exists over the northern Pacific Ocean, often known as the 'Aleutian Low'.

The Moon's Phases and Ages 2025

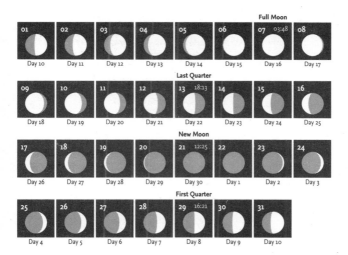

01	02	03	04	05	06	**Full Moon** 07 03:48	08
Day 10	Day 11	Day 12	Day 13	Day 14	Day 15	Day 16	Day 17

Last Quarter

New Moon

First Quarter

Air mass
A large volume of air that has uniform properties (particularly temperature and humidity) throughout. Air masses arise when air stagnates over a particular area for a long time. These areas are known as 'source regions' and are generally the semi-permanent high-pressure zones, which are the sub-tropical and polar anticyclones. The primary classification is based on temperature, giving Arctic (A), polar (P) and tropical (T) air.

O

October – In This Month

8 October 1903 – Heavy rain hit north-east England during what was the wettest month in England and Wales since records began. An average of 218 millimetres fell over the course of the month, 268 per cent of the long-term average, and by the end of the month over 10,000 hectares of the country was under flood water.

17 October 1922 – SS *Hopelyn* foundered and sank on Scroby Sands off the Norfolk coast after being blown off course by a strong gale, which broke the ship's steering gear. The wreck lies at a depth of only 2 metres.

19 October 1880 – Unseasonably early snow fell on London and the south of England, with the *Diss Express* describing it as 'an unbidden and therefore unwelcome guest'.

19 October 2023 – Storm Babet brought heavy rain to eastern Scotland, where some places saw over 100 millimetres of rain in 24 hours. Angus received 343.2 millimetres of rain over the month, or 386 per cent of the long-term average.

21 October 2001 – 82.2 millimetres of rain fell at Cambridge, leading to localised flooding in the Fens.

24 October 1896 – Early snowfall was recorded in Northern Ireland, at the end of a cold month. There hasn't been a colder October since.

24 October 1999 – High winds caused 20 metres of the Grade II listed Bognor Regis pier to collapse into the sea.

28 October 1996 – The remnants of Hurricane Lili hit the south-west of England, breaching the coastal pebble ridge at Porlock Bay and allowing seawater to flood the low-lying marshes behind.

O

Royal National Lifeboat Institution

On 6 October 1822, HMS *Vigilant*, which had been sheltering from a storm in Douglas Bay in the Isle of Man, put to sea, because the captain believed the wind and waves had abated. The vessel was blown onto Conister Rock. Observing the wreck from his house onshore, Sir William Hillary rapidly organised two craft to rescue the sailors, and eventually 97 were brought ashore. Later that year, a ship that had been sent to escort the damaged *Vigilant* back to England sank and three rescuers were drowned. These incidents gave Sir William the germ of an idea for an organisation that would design, build and maintain lifeboats around the shores of Great Britain.

Painting of Sir William Hillary.

The latest type of all-weather lifeboat to be operated by the RNLI is the Shannon class, with Scarborough's Frederic William Plaxton *pictured here.*

In February 1823, Sir William issued an appeal leaflet for such an institution to be set up. By the following year, the appeal had gathered support and a meeting was held at the London Tavern in Bishopsgate. Thus, in March 1824, The National Institution for the Preservation of Life from Shipwreck was established with the King, George IV, as patron. Although sources disagree on the exact date, sometime around 1860 the organisation gained a royal charter and added 'Royal' to its name. Over the next year the organisation built 13 new lifeboat stations and amassed a fleet of 15 boats. On 5 October 1854 (after one other name change), the organisation was renamed the Royal National Lifeboat Institution (RNLI) by which name it is still known.

Nowadays, the organisation maintains over 200 lifeboat stations and more than 400 lifeboats. It is unique in that it is maintained solely by voluntary contributions and its crew (over 9,000) are all volunteers.

O

The Institution has saved more than 140,000 lives since its foundation, for the loss of about 600 crew members. Some of these rescues have become the stuff of legend. One of the legendary coxswains was Henry Blogg of Cromer. He was awarded the George Cross and the British Empire Medal as well as the Institution's gold medal three times and silver four times. He served the Institution for 53 years, and in that time, with his crews he rescued 873 lives. He is known as 'The greatest of all lifeboatmen' and 'One of the bravest men who ever lived'.

It may be said that the RNLI owes its very existence to the severe weather in October 1822.

November

Introduction

November often continues where October left off. It's likely to remain unsettled as a succession of low-pressure systems push eastwards. Strong winds and heavy rain may cause disruption at times. If the ground is already saturated with water, then flooding can become an issue, exacerbated by fallen leaves blocking drains. The year 2009 saw the wettest November on record for the UK, with severe gales and flooding recorded across Britain and Ireland. The rain from 16–19 November was so relentless that a weather station in Cumbria saw the most rainfall ever recorded in four consecutive days at 495 millimetres, that's just over 19 inches of rain.

As November progresses, quieter and more anticyclonic interludes are more likely to develop. This see-sawing between cyclonic and anticyclonic conditions is a key feature of the last of Lamb's five natural seasons – the 'early winter' season, which spans from 20 November to 19 January. With the weather frequently coming from the west, it is mostly quite mild, although cold snaps are possible between depressions.

Although high pressure provides a break from unsettled, westerly driven weather, it comes with its own set of risks. Mist and fog are a classic autumnal feature. Fog, which is essentially just water droplets suspended in the air, is defined by the Met Office as reducing visibility below 1 kilometre. Meanwhile mist, which is not quite as dense, brings visibility between 1 and 8 kilometres. Both are common on chilly autumn mornings and can be slow to clear.

Generally, air temperatures must rise for fog to dissipate, with energy from the Sun heating the water droplets enough until they evaporate back into water vapour. Although they are improving, computer models often struggle to forecast this. A more amateur technique that can be used during these autumn months involves taking the month you are in, and then adding two, to get the time of fog clearance. With November being the eleventh month, this method suggests fog may not clear until 1 p.m. However, fog can also be cleared by strengthening winds.

As the weather turns colder, freezing fog may also be an issue. It forms the same way as regular fog, but as the name suggests, under freezing temperatures. The droplets of water in the air become 'supercooled', but don't fully freeze while suspended in air, as they need a surface to freeze onto. When the foggy air comes into contact with an object, it leaves a deposit of ice crystals, known as rime.

N

Weather Extremes in November

Country	Temp.	Location	Date
Maximum temperature			
England	21.1°C	Chelmsford (Essex) Clacton (Essex) Cambridge (Cambridgeshire) Mildenhall (Suffolk)	5 Nov 1938
Wales	22.4°C	Trawsgoed (Ceredigion)	1 Nov 2015
Scotland	20.6°C	Edinburgh Royal Botanic Garden & Liberton (Edinburgh)	4 Nov 1946
Northern Ireland	18.5°	Murlough (County Down)	3 Nov 1979 1 Nov 2007 and 10 Nov 2015
Minimum temperature			
England	-16.1°C	Scaleby (Cumbria)	30 Nov 1912
Wales	-18.0°C	Llysdinam (Powys)	28 Nov 2010
Scotland	-23.3°C	Braemar (Aberdeenshire)	14 Nov 1919
Northern Ireland	-12.2°C	Lisburn (County Antrim)	15 Nov 1919

Country	Pressure	Location	Date
Maximum pressure			
Scotland	1046.7 hPa	Aviemore (Inverness-shire)	10 Nov 1999
Minimum pressure			
Scotland	939.7 hPa	Monach Lighthouse (Outer Hebrides)	11 Nov 1877

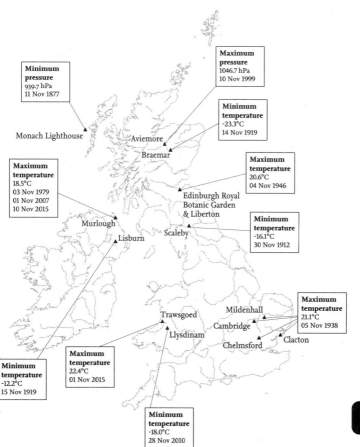

Minimum pressure
939.7 hPa
11 Nov 1877

Monach Lighthouse

Maximum pressure
1046.7 hPa
10 Nov 1999

Minimum temperature
-23.3°C
14 Nov 1919

Aviemore

Braemar

Maximum temperature
18.5°C
03 Nov 1979
01 Nov 2007
10 Nov 2015

Maximum temperature
20.6°C
04 Nov 1946

Edinburgh Royal Botanic Garden & Liberton

Murlough

Lisburn

Scaleby

Minimum temperature
-16.1°C
30 Nov 1912

Trawsgoed

Mildenhall

Cambridge

Llysdinam

Chelmsford

Clacton

Maximum temperature
21.1°C
05 Nov 1938

Minimum temperature
-12.2°C
15 Nov 1919

Maximum temperature
22.4°C
01 Nov 2015

Minimum temperature
-18.0°C
28 Nov 2010

N

The Weather in November 2023

Observation	Location	Date
Max. temperature 16.7°C	Writtle (Essex)	13 November
Min. temperature -7.7°C	Shap (Cumbria)	25 November
Most rainfall 124.2 mm	Honister Pass (Cumbria)	13 November
Highest gust 78 mph (125 kph/68 kt)	Langdon Bay (Kent)	2 November
Greatest snow depth 10 cm	Copley (Durham)	30 November

Unsettled weather driven by low pressure systems arriving from the Atlantic continued to be the norm in early November, with the jet stream displaced to the south of normal. On the 1st and 2nd Storm Ciarán raged across Europe, with seven people dying in Tuscany and extensive damage reported in the Channel Islands and northern France, but southern England was spared the worst effects. Nevertheless, the port of Dover was closed and cross-Channel ferry services suspended, and up to 150,000 properties lost power. The incredibly rough sea conditions meant a major incident was declared in Hampshire and the Isle of Wight, with coastal properties damaged, several vehicles swept into the sea by waves, and flights and rail services cancelled.

Storm Debi followed on the 13th, with Northern Ireland, North Wales and north-west England bearing the brunt this time. Gusts of 77 mph (124 kph/70 knots) were recorded along the Welsh coast, and the Met Office issued amber warnings for parts of Northern Ireland, Cumbria, Lancashire and Merseyside. As well as high winds, these systems brought yet more rain, adding to what had already been a very wet autumn. Storm Debi brought as much as 100 millimetres of rain to some upland areas, and localised flooding caused disruption to roads and rail services in southern Scotland.

Temperatures dropped gradually during the middle of the month, with -7.1°C recorded at Altnaharra on the 16th and frosts across England on the 12th, but were not too extreme for the time of year. From the 15th the weather was calmer, while the continued Atlantic influence kept temperatures mild.

Towards the end of the month, high pressure of the south-west signalled a change in weather type; more northerly airflow brought drier weather and a sudden drop in temperatures. Northern and eastern areas saw some snow as precipitation arrived from the North Sea, and even as far south as Dorset temperatures fell to almost -5°C.

Overall, temperature and rainfall were both near average for the time of year. Northern and western Scotland were slightly colder and drier than normal, due to a low pressure anomaly extending west from Germany and Denmark to eastern England and Scotland. Southern England was generally warmer and wetter than expected. Sunshine hours were slightly above average at 112 per cent, but parts of Wales and south-west England were considerably duller.

N

Sunrise and Sunset 2025

Location	Date	Rise	Azimuth °	Set	Azimuth °
Belfast					
	1 Nov (Sat)	07:26	114	16:47	245
	11 Nov (Tue)	07:46	120	16:28	240
	21 Nov (Fri)	08:05	125	16:13	235
	30 Nov (Sun)	08:21	128	16:03	232
Cardiff					
	1 Nov (Sat)	07:06	113	16:45	247
	11 Nov (Tue)	07:24	118	16:28	242
	21 Nov (Fri)	07:41	122	16:15	238
	30 Nov (Sun)	07:54	125	16:07	235
Edinburgh					
	1 Nov (Sat)	07:20	115	16:31	245
	11 Nov (Tue)	07:41	121	16:11	239
	21 Nov (Fri)	08:01	126	15:55	234
	30 Nov (Sun)	08:17	130	15:44	230
London					
	1 Nov (Sat)	06:54	113	16:33	247
	11 Nov (Tue)	07:11	118	16:16	242
	21 Nov (Fri)	07:28	122	16:03	238
	30 Nov (Sun)	07:42	125	15:55	235

Note that all times are in Universal Time (UT), otherwise known as Greenwich Mean Time (GMT). These times do not take Summer Time (BST) into account.

Moonrise and Moonset 2025

Location	Date	Rise	Azimuth °	Set	Azimuth °
Belfast					
	1 Nov (Sat)	15:20	100	01:24	253
	11 Nov (Tue)	22:25	57	14:02	306
	21 Nov (Fri)	10:04	142	16:01	217
	30 Nov (Sun)	13:43	82	01:53	272
Cardiff					
	1 Nov (Sat)	15:05	100	01:19	254
	11 Nov (Tue)	22:27	60	13:36	303
	21 Nov (Fri)	09:27	137	16:15	222
	30 Nov (Sun)	13:34	83	01:41	272
Edinburgh					
	1 Nov (Sat)	15:10	101	01:10	253
	11 Nov (Tue)	22:07	56	13:58	308
	21 Nov (Fri)	10:06	145	15:36	214
	30 Nov (Sun)	13:30	82	01:42	272
London					
	1 Nov (Sat)	14:53	100	01:06	254
	11 Nov (Tue)	22:14	60	13:24	304
	21 Nov (Fri)	09:14	137	16:03	222
	30 Nov (Sun)	13:22	83	01:28	272

N

Note that all times are in Universal Time (UT), otherwise known as Greenwich Mean Time (GMT). These times do not take Summer Time (BST) into account.

Twilight Diagrams 2025

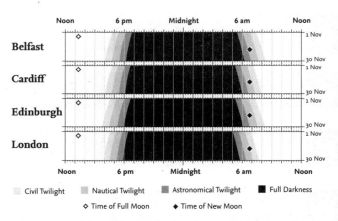

The exact times of the Moon's major phases are shown on the diagrams opposite.

Sea breeze

A flow of air from the sea onto the land. The land heats more rapidly than the sea, so the air above it rises, drawing cooler air off the sea. There is a corresponding flow towards the sea at altitude. The air rises along a 'sea-breeze front', which may lie many kilometres inland, depending on the local geography.

The Moon's Phases and Ages 2025

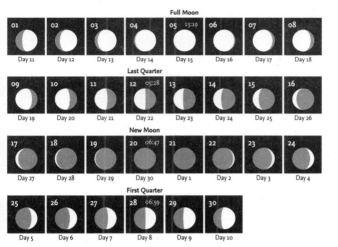

Full Moon

01	02	03	04	05 13:19	06	07	08
Day 11	Day 12	Day 13	Day 14	Day 15	Day 16	Day 17	Day 18

Last Quarter

09	10	11	12 05:28	13	14	15	16
Day 19	Day 20	Day 21	Day 22	Day 23	Day 24	Day 25	Day 26

New Moon

17	18	19	20 06:47	21	22	23	24
Day 27	Day 28	Day 29	Day 30	Day 1	Day 2	Day 3	Day 4

First Quarter

25	26	27	28 06:59	29	30
Day 5	Day 6	Day 7	Day 8	Day 9	Day 10

Land breeze

A flow of air from the land towards the sea. At night, the land cools more quickly than the sea. The denser air flows out towards the sea. A 'land-breeze front' is sometimes marked (especially on satellite images) by a line of cumulus cloud, where the air rises to flow back towards the land at altitude.

N

November – In This Month

1 November 1880 – Alfred Wegener, climatologist and inventor of the theory of continental drift, was born.

7 November 2015 – Storm Abigail was the first storm to be officially named by the UK Met Office and the Irish Met Éireann.

11 November 1099 – A storm surge in the North Sea was recorded by the *Anglo-Saxon Chronicle*, and dubbed the 'Martinmas Storm'. According to legend, before this storm the Goodwin Sands were an inhabited island, but the defences were washed away leaving the sand bar in its present state, where it remains a hazard to shipping off the Kent coast.

11 November 1919 – A snowstorm occurred across a large part of the UK, with 20 centimetres of snow falling in Edinburgh, 30 centimetres over Dartmoor and 43 centimetres at Balmoral.

14–15 November 1965 – A cold snap hit the country, with Kew to the south-west of London recording the coldest consecutive days so early in the winter since 1887. Power cuts affected large portions of the country after the Central Electricity Generating Board under-anticipated the cold weather and did not prepare enough generating capacity.

24 November 1938 – High winds swept across England at speeds of up to 108 mph (174 kph/94 knots), with 13 people reported killed and several small steamers blown ashore.

27 November 1701 – Birth of Anders Celsius. In 1742 he proposed the centigrade scale for temperature. Although the scale he originally proposed was inverted, in 1743 Jean-Pierre Christin suggested reversing it. In 1948 the scale was renamed in honour of Celsius by the International Committee for Weights and Measures.

28 November 1772 – Luke Howard was born, who in an 1802 lecture proposed the system for classifying and naming cloud types that is still used today. His lecture was published as an essay in 1803.

N

Snow

Snow is not unheard of in November, although outside of Scotland, a widespread covering is fairly rare. While still technically an autumn month, temperatures are falling as winter approaches. However, sub-zero temperatures are not a requirement, as the heaviest snowfall in the UK tends to fall when air temperatures are between zero and 2°C. This is due to the way snowflakes form. These are composed of tiny ice

A satellite image showing the extent of snow cover across Britain and Ireland following snow in late November 2010.

crystals, which become stuck together, eventually becoming heavy enough that they fall to the ground. If they descend through air that is slightly above freezing, they begin to melt around the edges, which allows them to form even bigger flakes. This is known as wet snow and it is the perfect kind for making snowballs, as it sticks together easily.

November 2010 brought the UK's earliest widespread winter snowfall since 1993. It began around 24 November. With high pressure established between Iceland and Greenland, and low pressure centred close to the Baltic states, the UK found itself in the path of very cold air from the Arctic and Siberia. What started as snow showers soon developed into something more widespread, as a series of fronts and troughs brought areas of persistent and heavy snow. As December approached, most parts of Britain and Ireland found themselves beneath lying snow. The worst affected places were eastern Scotland and north-east England, where snow accumulations of more than 50 centimetres were recorded.

Another notable cold snap in late November brought snow as far south as London and Cornwall, during the world's coldest year on record, 1904. A deep depression had moved eastwards across the country, clearing into the North Sea and bringing cold Arctic air to Britain and Ireland on the resultant north to north-easterly winds. Southern Scotland and northern England saw the most snow, with depths of around 46 centimetres. Elsewhere, most of the UK was covered in 2 to 5 centimetres of snow, although some reports suggest up to 18 centimetres of snow fell in Liskeard, Cornwall.

Globally, the 20 coldest years on record all occurred at least 90 years ago, with the most recent being 1929, which is the thirteenth coldest on record. Meanwhile, the world's top 20 warmest years on record have all occurred in the twenty-first century. More evidence, if it were needed, of our warming planet. While it is clear that heatwaves, wildfires and droughts will become more frequent, the effect on snowfall is much less clear. Even during 2023, the warmest year on record at the time of writing, November still saw 10 centimetres of snow falling in Durham.

N

December

Introduction

December heralds the beginning of meteorological winter but is likely to see little change in terms of weather patterns – at least in the first few weeks. Atlantic westerlies generally continue to dominate, bringing depressions interspersed with transient ridges of high pressure. The word 'winter' originates from the German 'wintar', which is connected with the word 'wed', meaning 'wet'. December fits this description nicely, as it is typically the wettest month of the year. However, it is not the coldest, as the chilliest weather is more likely to develop in January or February. Although the media will be paying very close attention to the chances of a white Christmas, it is actually more likely to snow at Easter. This is a somewhat tenuous statistic, as the timing of Easter varies year on year, but does at least support the idea that snow is more likely later in winter. Cold spells are still possible, but rarely last longer than a few days, thanks to a strong westerly flow.

In autumn, the temperature difference between the land and sea is relatively unimportant in determining the weather, whereas now, the surrounding oceans are warmer than the land, and can have more of an effect. Much like how showers develop as the Sun warms the land in summer, the relatively warm seas can cause showers and even thunderstorms to develop overhead, and over nearby coastal areas.

When a thunderstorm does develop at this time of year, and temperatures are sufficiently cold, an unusual phenomenon known as thundersnow can occur. It can cause quite a stir, especially when it develops over land. In December 2020, the city of Edinburgh woke to loud bangs and Police Scotland received calls from concerned residents, convinced they had heard explosions. In fact, the loud rumbles were thunderclaps distorted by the falling snow. The snow also helps to restrict the noise of the thunder, limiting the sound to around 3–5 kilometres from the lightning strike and causes the lightning to appear brighter as it reflects off the snowflakes, especially at night.

December's Full Moon in 2025 will be known as a 'Super Cold Moon'. You'd be forgiven for worrying that it might be the sign of a cold winter to come! In fact, it is named the 'Cold Moon' because it falls in the first month of meteorological winter and 'Super' because the Moon is at perigee. This means it is at the point in its orbit (which is not perfectly circular, but elliptical) that is closest to the Earth, which makes it appear slightly bigger and brighter.

The winter solstice (21 December 2025) brings the shortest day of the year and marks the start of astronomical winter. In the UK there are almost nine fewer daylight hours on this day compared to the summer solstice.

D

Weather Extremes in December

Country	Temp.	Location	Date
Maximum temperature			
England	17.7°C	Chivenor (Devon) Penkridge (Staffordshire)	2 Dec 1985 11 Dec 1994
Wales	18.0°C	Aber (Gwynedd)	18 Dec 1972
Scotland	18.7°C	Achafry (Sutherland)	28 Dec 2019
Northern Ireland	16.7°C	Ballykelly (County Londonderry)	2 Dec 1948
Minimum temperature			
England	-25.2°C	Shawbury (Shropshire)	13 Dec 1981
Wales	-22.7°C	Corwen (Denbighshire)	13 Dec 1981
Scotland	-27.2°C	Altnaharra (Highland)	30 Dec 1995
Northern Ireland	-18.7°C	Castlederg (County Tyrone)	24 Dec 2010

Country	Pressure	Location	Date
Maximum pressure			
Scotland	1051.9 hPa	Wick (Caithness)	24 Dec 1926
Minimum pressure			
Northern Ireland	927.2 hPa	Belfast (County Antrim)	8 Dec 1886

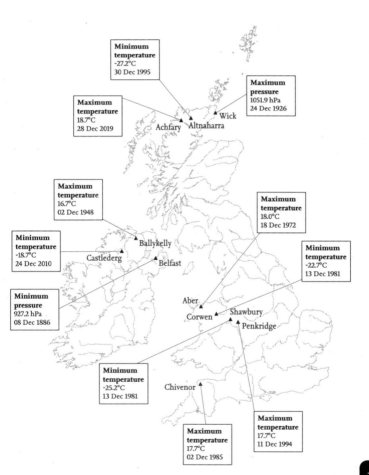

Minimum temperature
-27.2°C
30 Dec 1995

Maximum pressure
1051.9 hPa
24 Dec 1926

Maximum temperature
18.7°C
28 Dec 2019

Achfary Altnaharra Wick

Maximum temperature
16.7°C
02 Dec 1948

Maximum temperature
18.0°C
18 Dec 1972

Minimum temperature
-18.7°C
24 Dec 2010

Ballykelly

Castlederg

Belfast

Minimum temperature
-22.7°C
13 Dec 1981

Minimum pressure
927.2 hPa
08 Dec 1886

Aber

Corwen Shawbury

Penkridge

Minimum temperature
-25.2°C
13 Dec 1981

Chivenor

Maximum temperature
17.7°C
02 Dec 1985

Maximum temperature
17.7°C
11 Dec 1994

D

The Weather in December 2023

Observation	Location	Date
Max. temperature 16.1°C	Rhyl No. 2 (Glwyd)	23 December
Min. temperature -12.5°C	Altnaharra No. 2 (Sutherland)	3 December
Most rainfall 118.8 mm	Kinlochewe (Ross & Cromarty)	16 December
Highest gust 89 mph (143 kph/71 kt)	Fair Isle (Shetland)	27 December
Greatest snow depth 11 cm	Copley (Durham) Middleton, Hillside (Derbyshire)	3 December

The first week of December saw cold weather continue, with particularly low temperatures in northern Scotland and even Cornwall seeing minimums close to -5°C. Northern England saw heavy snowfall, with Cumbria and parts of Derbyshire particularly badly affected. The M6 was closed for a short period, and rest centres had to be opened to shelter stranded travellers. From the 9th, two successive Atlantic storms (Elin and Fergus), driven by a strong westerly jet stream, brought milder weather accompanied by high winds and rain. The worst effects were felt in the Republic of Ireland, but rail services were also disrupted in Yorkshire on the 10th and 11th, and on the 12th flooding in London saw vehicles stranded.

Thereafter, the rest of the month was mild, with only the far north seeing some cold weather continue. A succession of Atlantic fronts brought persistent rain, while on the 21st a system subsequently named Storm Pia by the Danish meteorological service brought high winds to Scotland and north-west England and Wales. Some bridges were closed to high-sided vehicles, and rail and ferry services were disrupted. In Shetland and the far north of Scotland, the same system brought heavy snow.

Christmas Day had the highest minimum temperature on record, with 12.4°C at Exeter Airport and East Malling in Kent. The rest of the month saw yet more unsettled weather, with Storm Gerrit causing significant disruption from the 27th to 29th. Northern Scotland was badly affected, with numerous stations recording winds over 81 mph (130 kph/70 knots) and snow trapping cars on the A9, while in Greater Manchester a tornado damaged around 100 homes. Yet another Atlantic front at the very end of the month only compounded the disruption.

With the exception of northern Scotland, December was warmer than average across the UK, by between 1.5 and 2.5°C. For England and Wales, this was the fifth-warmest December on record since 1884, with southern England particularly warm. It was also one of the wettest Decembers on record for the UK as a whole (the eighth wettest in a series from 1836). After a very wet autumn, areas in north-east England and northern and eastern Scotland that could have done without further rain received more than twice the average rainfall. Sunshine was less than 66 per cent of the average, and in parts of southern England was as low as 50 per cent, at only 26.6 hours across the whole month.

Exosphere
The name sometimes applied to the upper region of the thermosphere above an altitude of 200–700 km.

D

Sunrise and Sunset 2025

Location	Date	Rise	Azimuth °	Set	Azimuth °
Belfast					
	1 Dec (Mon)	08:22	128	16:02	231
	11 Dec (Thu)	08:36	131	15:57	229
	21 Dec (Sun)	08:44	132	15:59	228
	31 Dec (Wed)	08:46	131	16:07	229
Cardiff					
	1 Dec (Mon)	07:56	125	16:07	234
	11 Dec (Thu)	08:08	128	16:03	232
	21 Dec (Sun)	08:15	128	16:05	232
	31 Dec (Wed)	08:18	128	16:13	232
Edinburgh					
	1 Dec (Mon)	08:19	130	15:43	230
	11 Dec (Thu)	08:33	133	15:38	227
	21 Dec (Sun)	08:42	134	15:39	228
	31 Dec (Wed)	08:43	133	15:48	227
London					
	1 Dec (Mon)	07:44	125	15:54	234
	11 Dec (Thu)	07:56	128	15:51	232
	21 Dec (Sun)	08:03	128	15:53	232
	31 Dec (Wed)	08:06	128	16:01	232

Note that all times are in Universal Time (UT), otherwise known as Greenwich Mean Time (GMT). These times do not take Summer Time (BST) into account.

Moonrise and Moonset 2025

Location	Date	Rise	Azimuth °	Set	Azimuth °
Belfast					
	1 Dec (Mon)	13:52	70	03:23	285
	11 Dec (Thu)	–	–	12:38	279
		22:55	75		
	21 Dec (Sun)	10:31	141	16:46	220
	31 Dec (Wed)	12:46	44	05:43	314
Cardiff					
	1 Dec (Mon)	13:48	72	03:06	283
	11 Dec (Thu)	–	–	12:24	279
		22:49	76		
	21 Dec (Sun)	09:56	137	16:58	225
	31 Dec (Wed)	12:56	48	05:11	310
Edinburgh					
	1 Dec (Mon)	13:38	70	03:14	285
	11 Dec (Thu)	–	–	12:29	280
		22:41	74		
	21 Dec (Sun)	10:33	144	16:22	218
	31 Dec (Wed)	12:24	42	05:41	316
London					
	1 Dec (Mon)	13:36	72	02:53	283
	11 Dec (Thu)	23:52	86	12:12	279
	21 Dec (Sun)	09:43	137	16:45	225
	31 Dec (Wed)	12:43	48	04:58	310

Note that all times are in Universal Time (UT), otherwise known as Greenwich Mean Time (GMT). These times do not take Summer Time (BST) into account.

D

Twilight Diagrams 2025

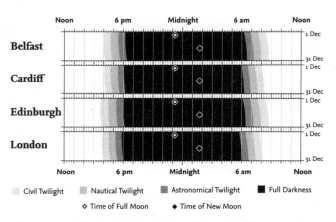

Civil Twilight   Nautical Twilight   Astronomical Twilight   Full Darkness

◇ Time of Full Moon   ◆ Time of New Moon

The exact times of the Moon's major phases are shown on the diagrams opposite.

Trade winds

There are two trade-wind zones, north and south of the equator, with the north-east trades and the south-east trades, respectively, where the air converges on the low-pressure region at the equator. The direction and strength of these winds do remain relatively constant throughout the year, and were thus a reliable source of motive power for sailing ships.

The Moon's Phases and Ages 2025

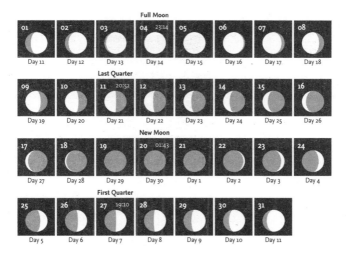

Full Moon

01	02	03	04 23:14	05	06	07	08
Day 11	Day 12	Day 13	Day 14	Day 15	Day 16	Day 17	Day 18

Last Quarter

09	10	11 20:52	12	13	14	15	16
Day 19	Day 20	Day 21	Day 22	Day 23	Day 24	Day 25	Day 26

New Moon

17	18	19	20 01:43	21	22	23	24
Day 27	Day 28	Day 29	Day 30	Day 1	Day 2	Day 3	Day 4

First Quarter

25	26	27 19:10	28	29	30	31
Day 5	Day 6	Day 7	Day 8	Day 9	Day 10	Day 11

Aurora

A luminous event occurring in the upper atmosphere between appoximately 100 and 1,000 km. It arises when energetic particles from the Sun raise atoms to higher energy levels. When the atoms drop back to their original energy level, they emit the characteristic green and red shades that are visible to human eyes (from oxygen and nitrogen, respectively).

D

December – In This Month

December 1740 – A major storm breached the flood defences at Dunwich, destroying most of what remained of the medieval city. In reality, it had been in decline for several hundred years before that, after an earlier storm caused the mouth of the river Blyth to move further north and continual erosion claimed successive streets and buildings.

1 December 1806 – The new Flamborough Head Lighthouse in Yorkshire was lit for the first time, and the first to use a coloured light (red) as part of its distinctive light pattern. It replaced an earlier structure on the same site, built in 1669, but never lit.

4 December 1816 – Riots erupted in Dundee over food shortages at the end of the 'year without a summer', which was caused by the 1815 eruption of Mount Tambora. The riots were exacerbated by the unpopularity of the Corn Laws that had been introduced the previous year.

13 December 1981 – A depression brought snow and high winds, with a storm surge up the Bristol Channel leading to extensive flooding. Temperatures were also extremely low, with parts of Shropshire recording lows of -25°C that night. Snow blocking roads in the Cotswolds meant the Queen had to stay the night in a local hotel.

18 December 1995 – A high pressure zone settled over Greenland, driving cold Arctic air south. This led to blizzards on Christmas Eve and Christmas Day, with four consecutive nights from the 26th onwards seeing lows of below -20°C. At Altnaharra a new December record was set at -27.2°C shortly after midnight on the 30th.

25 December 1896 – One of the mildest Christmas Days of the nineteenth century saw a high of 15.6°C recorded.

25 December 1927 – A blizzard covered the Midlands and Wales on perhaps the snowiest Christmas Day of the twentieth century. The snow continued over southern England into Boxing Day, with drifts of up to 6 metres reported in the Chilterns and 7.6 metres on Salisbury Plain.

31 December 1911 – The warmest New Year's Eve on record was measured at Colwyn Bay, where 16.8°C was measured.

D

El Niño

Over time, the surface waters of the tropical eastern Pacific Ocean warm and cool. The warm phase was first noticed by fishermen off the coast of Peru, and named 'El Niño' by locals, which translates to 'the boy'. Since El Niño usually peaks in December, around Christmastime, it is thought to have originated from 'El Niño de Navidad', named after the newborn Christ. Meanwhile, the cold phase is called 'La Niña' – 'the girl'. El Niño and La Niña are opposite phases in a phenomenon known as the El Niño Southern Oscillation. The phases alternate in an irregular cycle, with El Niño occurring every 2–7 years.

Normally, trade winds blow westwards. When El Niño develops, these winds weaken, or even reverse, and warm surface waters spread eastwards across the Pacific Ocean. The influx of warm water triggers atmospheric convection, bringing increased rainfall to the normally dry lands of Ecuador and northern Peru. On the other side of the Pacific, the reduction in sea surface temperatures brings drought to Indonesia and eastern Australia.

La Niña brings the reverse of this. Strengthening trade winds cause a process called 'upwelling' off the coast of South America, where cold, nutrient-rich water is brought to the surface of the tropical eastern Pacific. During this phase, the weather here becomes drier. Meanwhile, warmer waters in the western Pacific bring flooding to the islands of Indonesia, New Guinea and parts of Australia.

The El Niño Southern Oscillation doesn't just affect countries neighbouring the Pacific. Through what meteorologists call 'teleconnections', El Niño and La Niña can have knock-on effects around the world.

Facing page: *Increased rainfall during the winter of 1997–98, caused by an El Niño event, led to dramatic flooding and erosion in Peru, as pictured here.*

In 2023, an El Niño event was declared, reaching its peak in December of the same year, and continuing into January 2024, before gradually easing. As El Niño brings unusually warm surface waters across the Pacific, global temperatures typically increase during this phase. Climate scientists confirmed that 2023 was the hottest year on record, driven by human-induced warming, but likely boosted by the effects of El Niño.

Here in the UK, the response of our weather to El Niño is complicated. Some scientists associate El Niño with a wet and windy start to our winters, and a colder end, while La Niña is said to bring the opposite. The link between El Niño and our summer temperatures is even more tenuous. In the past, extreme summer heat has occurred during both El Niño and La Niña. In fact, the UK recorded its highest temperature on record during a La Niña episode, when 40.3°C was observed in Lincolnshire on 19 July 2022.

D

Additional Information

The Regional Climates of Britain

1   South-West England and the Channel Islands

The south-western region may be taken to include Cornwall, Devon, Somerset, Gloucestershire, Dorset and the western portion of Wiltshire. This area is largely dominated by its proximity to the sea, although the northern and eastern portion of the region, being farther from the sea, often experiences rather different weather. In many respects the closeness of the Atlantic means that the weather resembles that encountered in the west of Ireland or the Hebrides. Generally, the climate is extremely mild, although that in the Scilly Isles is drier, sunnier and much milder than the closest part of the Cornish peninsula, just 40 km farther north. In the prevailing moist, south-westerly airstreams, the Scilly Isles are not only surrounded by the sea, but they are fairly flat with no hills to cause the air to rise and produce rain. The Channel Islands, by contrast, well to the east, are affected by their proximity to France and sometimes come under the influence of anticyclonic high-pressure conditions on the near Continent, so their overall climate tends to be more extreme.

Despite its generally mild weather, the region has experienced extremes, such as the exceptional snowfall in March 1891 that paralysed southern counties and introduced the word 'blizzard' to descriptions of British weather. The region also experienced the British rainstorm record of 279 mm in one single observational day (09.00 am one day to 08.59 am the next) occurring on 18 July 1955 at Martinstown in Dorset.

Most of the peninsula of Devon and Cornwall sees very few days of frost and some areas are almost completely frost-free. Temperatures are lower, of course, over the high ground of Bodmin Moor and Dartmoor. Indeed, those areas and the Mendip Hills and Blackdown Hills do all have slightly different climatic regimes. The influence of the Severn Estuary extends well inland, and actually has an affect on the weather in the Midlands (see page 218). In winter, it allows mild air to penetrate far inland. In Cornwall and Devon, particularly in summer, sea breezes from opposite sides of the peninsula converge over the high ground that runs along the centre of the peninsula, leading to the formation of major cumulonimbus

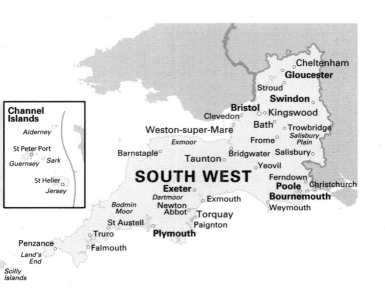

clouds and frequent showers, which may give extreme rainfall. It was this that led to the Lynmouth disaster in August 1952, when waters from a flash flood devastated the town and caused the deaths of 34 people. A somewhat similar situation arose in August 2004 in nearby Boscastle and Crackington Haven, although in that instance, no lives were lost.

The escarpment of the Cotswolds, overlooking the Severn valley, often proves to be a boundary between different types of weather. This is particularly the case when there is a north-westerly wind. Then heavy showers may affect areas on the high ground, while it is warmer and with less wind over the flatter land in the Severn valley and around Gloucester. It is often bitterly cold on the high ground above the escarpment.

2   South-East England and East Anglia

The weather in the south-eastern corner of the country may be divided into two main areas: the counties along the south coast (Hampshire, West and East Sussex and Kent); and the Home Counties around London, and East Anglia, although East Anglia (Norfolk and Sufflok in particular) often experiences rather different conditions to the Home Counties.

The coastal strip from Hampshire (including the Isle of Wight) eastwards to southern Kent has long been recognised as the warmest and sunniest part of the British Isles. This largely arises from the longer duration of warm tropical air from the Continent when compared with the length of time that such air penetrates to more northern areas. The coastal strip from Norfolk to northern Kent does experience some warming effect when the winds are in the prevailing south-westerly direction, offsetting the cold effects produced by the North Sea. This coast may experience severe weather when there is an easterly or north-easterly airflow over the North Sea. This is particularly the case in winter: cold easterly winds bring significant snowfall to the region. It is also a feature of spring and early summer when temperatures are reduced when there is an onshore wind off the North Sea.

Frosts and frost hollows are a feature of the South and North Downs, the Chiltern Hills (in Berkshire, Bedfordshire and

Hertfordshire), and in the high ground in East Anglia. Here, the chalk subsoil loses heat by night as do the sandy soils of Surrey and Breckland in Norfolk, leading to ground frost in places in any month of the year.

Along the south coast there is a tendency for most rain to fall in the autumn and winter, whereas for the rest of the region (the Home Counties and East Anglia) precipitation tends to occur more-or-less equally throughout the year. Because of the reliance upon groundwater, the whole region sometimes suffers from drought, when winter rains (in particular) have been insufficient to recharge the underground reserves.

3 The Midlands

The Midlands region consists of a very large number of counties: Shropshire, Herefordshire, Worcestershire, Warwickshire, West Midlands, Staffordshire, Nottinghamshire, Lincolnshire, Leicestershire, Rutland, Northamptonshire and the southern part of Derbyshire (excluding the high ground of the High Peak in the north). Of all the regions of the British Isles, this is naturally the area which has the least maritime influence. The region has been likened to a shallow bowl surrounded by hills (the Welsh Marches, the Cotswolds, the Northamptonshire Escarpment, the Derbyshire Peak and the Staffordshire Moorlands) and with a slight dome in the centre (the Birmingham Plateau). In winter the warmest area is that closest to the Severn Valley, where warm south-westerly winds may penetrate inland, whereas in summer the warmest region lies to the north-east, farthest from those moderating winds. Yet the western area is also prone to very cold nights in autumn, winter and early spring. (The lowest temperature ever recorded in England was -26.1°C at Newport in Shropshire on 10 January 1982.) Frosts are a feature of the whole region, partly because of the sandy nature of most of the soils and also because of the lack of maritime influence.

Precipitation is fairly evenly spread across the region, although the west, along the Welsh border and the high northern area of the High Peak, experiences the highest rainfall. The east (Lincolnshire and the low ground in the

east of Nottinghamshire and Northamptonshire along the valleys of the Trent and Nene) tends to be drier. Because of the rain-shadow created by the Welsh mountains, over which considerable rainfall occurs, some areas of the west of this Midlands region are drier than might otherwise be expected. There is some increase in rainfall over the slightly higher ground of the Birmingham Plateau and also towards the south and the Cotswold hills. Towards East Anglia there is a strong tendency for most rain to occur in summer, when showers are most numerous. In the very hilly areas on the Welsh border and in the Peak District, the wettest months are December and January. The Derbyshire Peak and the Staffordshire Moorlands tend to experience considerable snowfall in winter, as do high areas of the Welsh Marches. On the lower ground to the east, snowfall is greater in the year than in the west. This is particularly the case when there are easterly or north-easterly winds that penetrate inland and bring snow from the North Sea.

4 North-West England and the Isle of Man

The North-West region consists of the land west of the Pennine chain, that is Cumbria and Lancashire in particular, especially including the mountainous Lake District in Cumbria, but also extends south to include Merseyside, Greater Manchester, Cheshire and the western side of Derbyshire. The region's weather tends to be mild and wetter in winter than regions to the east of the Pennines, and cooler in summer than regions to the south. It was, of course, the mild, relatively damp climate that was responsible for the region being the centre for the spinning of cotton, in contrast to the wool handled in the drier east. The maritime influence is seen in the fact that coastal areas are often warmer in winter and cooler in summer than areas farther inland.

There is a great difference in the amount of precipitation between the north and south of this region. The north, in Cumbria and the Lake District is notorious for high rainfall. Honister Pass, in the Lake District, currently holds the record for rainfall in 24 hours and is the wettest inhabited location

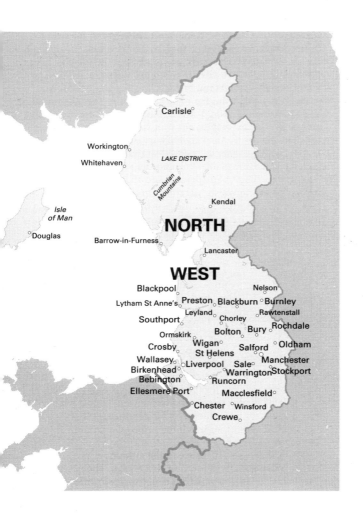

in Britain. The extreme rainfall has often contributed to severe flooding, such as that in 2005 and 2009 in Carlisle, Cockermouth, Workington, Appleby and Keswick. By contrast, rainfall is much less over the Cheshire plain, which like much of Merseyside, actually lies in the rain shadow of the Welsh mountains and is thus much drier.

The prevailing wind from the south-west may give very high wind speeds over the high ground of the Pennines, while an easterly wind may produce the only named British wind, the visciously strong, and noisy, Helm wind, as air cascades over the escarpment west of Cross Fell and over the Eden valley in the north of Cumbria.

Most years see some early snow in autumn on the high fells, and in the north on the high ground it may be persistent, although it rarely lasts throughout the winter. The low ground along the coast and in the south sees relatively little snow and what does fall remains lying for just a few days.

5 North-East England and Yorkshire

The region of North-East England is well-defined by two geographical boundaries. On the west is the Pennine range, on the east, the North Sea. The northern boundary may be taken as the river Tweed and the southern as the estuary of the Humber. The region includes very high moorland in the north and west. In general the ground slopes down from the Pennine chain towards the east coast. There are, however, considerable areas of lower land, such as that in parts of Northumberland and, in particular, in the south of Yorkshire. Because the prevailing winds in Britain are from the west, they tend to deposit most of their rainfall over the Pennines, so that there is a rain shadow effect that reaches right across this region to the coast, and the whole region is drier than might otherwise be expected. With westerly winds, the high fells also tend to break up the cloud cover, so that the whole area to the east is surprisingly sunny. On the other hand, the North Sea exerts a strong cooling effect, keeping general temperatures fairly low. The region is, however, open to easterly and northerly winds and tends to suffer from gales off

of any severe storms, not only does the island act as an 'early warning system' for the remainder of the British Isles, but also tends to temper their effects and reduce their severity for regions farther to the east.

Taken as a whole, the higher ground is located around the coasts of Ireland, with lower ground in the centre of the island. There is therefore a tendency for rainfall to be higher around the coasts than in the centre. One consequence of the warm sea is that in winter, in particular, the temperature difference between the cool land and the warm sea helps to strengthen developing depressions, so that frontal systems – and the rain that they bear – tend to be stronger in winter than in summer. Rainfall on hills close to the western coasts is greater at that time of the year, when there are also more showers, which add to the overall total amount of rain. This is particularly the case when unstable polar maritime air arrives in the wake of a depression. As it passes over the main flow of the North Atlantic Drift, it becomes strongly heated from below – sometimes by as much as 9 degrees Celsius – which thus increases its instability and the strength of the showers that are generated. All of which increases the rainfall.

As far as temperatures are concerned, there is very little variation across the island, although there tends to be a greater range in the north-east as compared with those prevailing over the south-west of Ireland. Distance from the coast also plays a part. The area with the greatest range of temperature is in southern Ulster, which experiences colder temperatures in late autumn and winter than areas along the southern and western coasts. From late spring until early autumn, maximum temperatures are higher in the north-east than in southern and western Ireland. In high summer, latitude does play a part, with temperatures being slightly higher in southern areas than along the north coast. One consequence of the equable maritime climate is that high temperatures, even in high summer, are rare, especially when compared with those that are experienced in southern England. On very rare occasions, in winter, the frigid air of the Siberian High may extend right across England and into Ireland and remains strong enough to overcome the influence of the warm air from the Atlantic. This was the case in 1962/1963 and in 2009/2010, but these winters were exceptional. Otherwise, frost is rare in coastal areas and occurs on just some 40 occasions in inland regions. As may be expected, snowfall is rare. Only in the extreme north-east does snow fall on an average of 30 days a year. In the far south-west, this figure decreases to about 5 days a year, and nowhere does snow lie for more than about a day or so.

The difference between the western coasts and the more sheltered inland areas is perhaps most obvious when wind strengths are compared. The strongest winds are observed on the northern coast of Ulster, which tends to be close to the area of the Atlantic over which depressions may undergo explosive deepening, with a consequent increase in wind speed. On rare occasions, such as the 'Night of the Big Wind', which began on the afternoon of 6 January 1839, highly destructive winds may extend right across the island, even into the far south.

8 Scotland

As with Wales, Scotland consists of several areas with diverse climates, which are a result of its mountainous as well as its maritime nature. Again as in the case with Wales, there are five distinct areas. Because they are at a distance from the mainland, the three island areas of the Hebrides (or Western Isles), Orkney and Shetland form one climatic area. In the west of the mainland, there is a distinction between the very mountainous Western Highlands region, running from Sutherland in the north, right the way down the west coast. The climate here is extremely wet because of the mountainous nature. To the east of this region, particularly in Caithness, Moray, and most of Aberdeenshire, although still a highland region (the Eastern Highlands), the area is shielded from the prevailing westerly winds by the Cairngorm Mountains and warmed by the föhn effect. It is, however, fully exposed to frigid northerly winds, especially in the north, in Caithness, and particularly so in winter. On the east coast farther to the south, the climate is essentially the same from the Moray Firth, down the coastal strip of Aberdeenshire, Angus, and Fife, across the Firth of Forth and as far as the eastern end of the Borders. Farther inland, the Central Lowlands and the western area of the Borders in Dumfries and Galloway and Ayrshire form yet another climatic region.

The highest temperatures are recorded in all areas in July (sometimes July and August in the outer islands), and there is a difference of some 2–3 degrees Celsius between the average temperature recorded in the Borders in the south and that found in the extreme north of the Eastern Highlands region (in Caithness). It is striking that the highest December and January temperatures in the whole of Britain have been recorded in northern Scotland. In both cases, the low temperatures occurred as a result of the föhn effect in the lee of high mountains. On 26 January 2003, Aboyne in Aberdeenshire saw a high of 18.3°C; on 28 December 2019 this was topped by a measurement of 18.7°C at Achfary in Sutherland. High temperatures tend to occur in the Western Highlands with southerly or south-easterly winds, whereas the highest in the Eastern Higlands occur with westerly winds. The lowest temperatures occur in December or January in all regions with the exception of the Hebrides, Orkney and Shetland, where the lowest temperatures are recorded in February. The lowest recorded temperature, -27.2°C, was measured at Braemar in Aberdeenshire on 10 January 1982, 1 Febuary 1895, and at Altnaharra in the Highlands on 30 December 1995. However, lower temperatures may have occurred at other locations where there are no recording stations.

Scotland is known for its wet climate. There is, however, quite a striking difference between rainfall in the west (about 1250 mm per year in the outer islands and even more in the Western Highlands region), and rainfall in the eastern coastal region (that running from the Moray Firth down to the Borders). Here, yearly totals of just 650–750 mm are typical. This key feature of the Scottish climate is, of course, related to the mountainous nature of the land on the west, which receives most of the precipitation and shields the rest of the country. Precipitation also falls as snow and, once again, there is a distinct difference between the west and east of the

country. Snowfall is also strongly dependent on altitude and here again the Western Highlands region receives greater amounts of snow than elsewhere. In the Western Isles and particularly in western Ayrshire, days on which snow is lying are very few.

When it comes to sunshine, the eastern coastal strip is favoured, as well as the area of the western edge of the Borders in the south. The sunniest areas in Scotland are northern Fife, the northern shore of the Firth of Tay and the Mull of Galloway. Here, sunshine totals may even match those found in southern England.

Thermopause
The transitional layer between the underlying mesosphere and the overlying exosphere. It is poorly defined and its altitude lies between 200 and 700 km, depending on solar activity.

Clouds

Altocumulus clouds.

Altocumulus

Altocumulus clouds (Ac) are medium-level clouds, with bases at 2–6 km, that, like all other varieties of cumulus, occur as individual, rounded masses. Although they may appear in small, isolated patches, they are normally part of extensive cloud sheets or layers and frequently form when gentle convection occurs within a layer of thin altostratus (page 234) breaking it up into separate heaps or rolls of cloud.

Altocumulus clouds may also take on the appearance of flat 'pancakes', but whatever the shape of the individual cloudlets, they always show some darker shading, unlike cirrocumulus. Blue sky is often visible between the separate masses of cloud – at least in the nearer parts of the layer.

Layers of altocumulus move as a whole, carried by the general wind at their height, but wind shear often causes the cloudlets to become arranged in long rolls or billows, which usually lie across the wind direction. High altocumulus or cirrocumulus of this type give rise to beautiful clouds that are commonly known as 'mackerel skies'.

Altostratus

Altostratus (As) is a dull, medium-level white or bluish-grey cloud in a relatively featureless layer, which may cover all or part of the sky. When illuminated by the rising or setting Sun, gentle undulations on the base may be seen, but these should not be confused with the regular ripples that often occur in altocumulus (page 233).

As with stratus, altocumulus may be created by gentle uplift. This frequently occurs at a warm front, where initial cirrostratus thickens and becomes altostratus, and the latter may lower and become rain-bearing nimbostratus (page 241). Patches or larger areas of altostratus may remain behind fronts, shower clouds or larger, organised storms. Conversely, altostratus may break up into altocumulus. Convection may then eat away at the cloud, until nothing is left.

Altostratus.

Cirrus.

Cirrus

Cirrus (Ci) is a wispy, thread-like cloud that normally occurs high in the atmosphere. Usually white, it may seem grey when seen against the light if it is thick enough.

Cirrus consists of ice crystals that are falling from slightly denser heads where the crystals are forming. In most cases wind speeds are higher at upper levels, so the heads move rapidly across the sky, leaving long trails of ice crystals behind them. Occasionally, the crystals fall into a deep layer of air moving at a steady speed. This can produce long, vertical trails of cloud.

Cirrocumulus

Cirrocumulus (Cc) is a very high white or bluish-white cloud, consisting of numerous tiny tufts or ripples, occurring in patches or larger layers that may cover a large part of the sky. The individual cloud elements are less than 1° across. They are sometime accompanied by fallstreaks of falling ice crystals. Unlike altocumulus (page 233) the small cloud elements do not show any shading. They are outlined by darker regions where the clouds are very thin or completely missing.

Cirrocumulus.

The cloud layer is often broken up into a regular pattern of ripples and billows. Clouds of this sort are often called a 'mackerel sky', although the term is sometimes applied to fine, rippled altocumulus. In fact, the differences between cirrocumulus and altocumulus are really caused only because the latter are lower and thus closer to the observer.

Cirrostratus
Cirrostratus (Cs) is a thin sheet of ice-crystal cloud and is most commonly observed ahead of the warm front of an approaching depression, when it is often the second cloud type to be noticed, after individual cirrus streaks. On many occasions, however, cirrostratus occurs as such a thin veil that it goes unnoticed, at least initially, until one becomes aware that the sky has lost its deep blue colour and has taken on a slightly milky appearance. The Sun remains clearly visible (and blindingly bright) through the cloud, but as the cirrostratus thickens, a slight drop in temperature may become apparent.

A solar halo in thin, almost invisible, cirrostratus cloud.

Once you realise that cirrostratus is present, it pays to check the sky frequently, because as it thickens it may display striking halo phenomena. This stage often passes fairly quickly as the cloud continues to thicken and lower towards the surface, eventually turning into thin altostratus (page 234).

Cirrostratus often has a fibrous appearance, especially if it arises from the gradual increase and thickening of individual cirrus streaks. Because the cloud is so thin, and contrast is low, the fibrous nature is easier to see when the Sun is hidden by lower, denser clouds or behind some other object.

Cumulus.

Cumulus

Cumulus clouds (Cu) are easy to recognise. They are the fluffy clouds that float across the sky on a fine day, and are often known as 'fair-weather clouds'. The individual heaps of cloud are generally well separated from one another – at least in their early stages. They have rounded tops and flat, darker bases. It is normally possible to see that these bases are all at one level. Together with stratus (page 241) and stratocumulus (page 242) they form closer to the ground than other cloud types.

The colour of cumulus clouds, like that of most other clouds, depends on how they are relative to the Sun and the observer. When illuminated by full sunlight, they are white – often blindingly white – but when seen against the Sun, unless they are very thin, they are various shades of grey.

Cumulonimbus

Cumulonimbus (Cb) is the largest and most energetic of the cumulus family. It appears as a vast mass of heavy, dense-looking cloud that normally reaches high into the sky. Its upper portion is usually brilliantly white in the sunshine, wheras its lower portions are very dark grey. Unlike the flat base of a cumulus, the bottom of a cumulonimbus is often ragged and it may even reach down to just above the ground. Shafts of precipitation are frequently clearly visible.

Cumulonimbus clouds consist of enormous numbers of individual convection cells, all growing rapidly up into the sky. Although cumulonimbus develop from tall cumulus, a critical difference is that at least part of their upper portions has changed from a hard 'cauliflower' appearance to a softer, more fibrous look. This is a sign that freezing has begun in the upper levels of the cloud.

Cumulonimbus.

Nimbostratus.

Stratus.

Nimbostratus

Nimbostratus (Nb) is a heavy, dark grey cloud with a very ragged base. It is the main rain-bearing cloud in many frontal systems. Shafts of precipitation (rain, sleet or snow) are visible below the cloud, which is often accompanied by tattered shreds of cloud that hang just below the base.

Just as cirrostratus often thickens and grades imperceptibly into altostratus, so the latter may thicken into nimbostratus. Once rain actually begins, or shafts of precipitation are seen to reach the ground, it is safe to call the cloud nimbostratus.

Stratus

Stratus (St) is grey, water-droplet cloud that usually has a fairly ragged base and top. It is always low and frequently shrouds the tops of buildings. Indeed it is identical to fog, which may be regarded as stratus at ground level. Although the cloud may be thin enough for the outline of the Sun to be seen clearly through it, in general it does not give rise to any optical phenomena. It forms under stable conditions and is one of the cloud types associated with 'anticyclonic gloom'.

Stratus may form either by gentle uplift (like the other stratiform clouds) or when nearly saturated air is carried by a gentle wind across a cold surface, which may be either land or sea. Normally low wind speeds favour its occurrence, because mixing is confined to a shallow layer near the ground. When there is a large temperature difference between the air and the surface, however, stratus may still occur, even with very strong winds. Stratus also commonly forms when a moist air-stream brings a thaw to a snow-covered surface.

There is very little precipitation from stratus, but it may produce a little drizzle or, when conditions are cold enough, even a few snow or ice grains. Ragged patches of stratus, called 'scud' by sailors, often form beneath rain clouds such as nimbostratus or cumulonimbus, especially where the humid air beneath the rain cloud is forced to rise slightly, such as when passing over low hills.

Stratocumulus

Stratocumulus (Sc) is a low, grey or whitish sheet of cloud, but unlike stratus it has a definite structure. There are distinct, separate masses of cloud that may be in the form of individual clumps, broader 'pancakes', or rolls. Sometimes these may be defined by thinner (and thus whitish) regions of cloud, but frequently blue sky is clearly visible between the masses of cloud.

Stratocumulus indicates stable conditions, and only slow changes to the current weather. It generally arises in one of two ways: either from the spreading out of cumulus clouds that reach an inversion, or through the break-up of a layer of stratus cloud. In the first case, the tops of the cumulus flatten and spread out sideways when they reach the inversion, producing clouds that are fairly even in thickness, with flat tops and bases. Initially, perhaps early in the day, there may be large areas of clear air, but the individual elements gradually merge to cover a larger area, or even completely blanket the sky.

In the second case, shallow convection (whose onset is often difficult to predict) begins within a sheet of stratus, causing the layer to break up. The regions of thinner cloud or clear air indicate where the air is descending, and the thicker, darker centres where it is rising.

Cloud heights

The height of clouds is usually given in feet (often with approximate metric equivalents). This may seem odd, when all other details of clouds, and meteorology in general, uses metric (SI) units. It is, however, a hangover from the way in which aircraft heights are specified. When aviation became general between the two World Wars, most commercial flying took place in the United Kingdom and America, so heights of aircraft and airfields were given in feet. It was obviously essential for cloud heights to be the same. The practice has continued: the heights of airfields, aircraft and clouds are still given in feet. The World Meteorological Organization recognises three ranges of cloud heights: low, middle and high. Clouds are specified by the height of their bases, not by that of their tops. The three divisions are:

Stratocumulus.

- Low clouds (bases 6,500 feet or lower, approx. 2 km and below): cumulus (page 238), stratocumulus (page 242), stratus (page 241).
- Middle clouds (bases between 6,500 and 20,000 feet, approx. 2 to 6 km): altocumulus (page 233), altostratus (page 234), nimbostratus (page 241).
- High clouds (bases over 20,000 feet, above 6 km): cirrus (page 235), cirrocumulus (page 235), cirrostratus (page 236).

One cloud type, cumulonimbus (page 239) commonly stretches through all three height ranges. Nimbostratus, although nominally a middle-level cloud, is frequently very deep and although it has a low base, may extend to much higher altitudes.

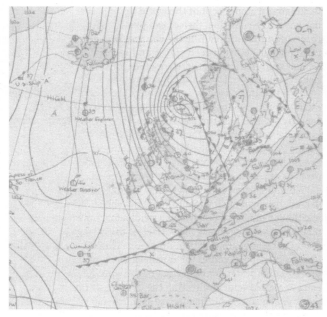

Met Office weather chart for 0600 UTC on 31 January 1953.

Storm Surges

With around 40 per cent of the world's population living within 100 km of the coastline, the sea can present a huge threat to coastal communities. While the ebb and flow of high and low tides and the cycle between spring and neap tides is generally regular and predictable, there are other factors that can cause a rise in sea level, endangering those living nearby.

Both tropical cyclones, such as hurricanes and typhoons, and extra-tropical cyclones, like those that affect the UK, have the capacity to bring destructive winds and torrential rainfall. But to coastal communities, they bring an additional threat: storm surges. As the name suggests, these are surges of water inland caused by storms. They can lead to devastating flooding and are perhaps one of the most dramatic weather events.

When the powerful winds within cyclones blow across the sea, they can push water towards the shore. However, the rotation of the Earth creates the Coriolis force, which means that as winds blow across the surface of the ocean, the water moves at an angle to the wind direction. This effect is known as Ekman Transport, and in the northern hemisphere the overall movement of water is to the right of the wind direction. So, for extra-tropical cyclones affecting the UK, the storm surge will generally be largest in the forward-right part of the storm.

Atmospheric pressure can also affect sea level. At the centre of a storm, where pressure is lowest, the 'inverse barometer effect' can 'pull' the water up, as if it were being sucked up by a straw. For every 1 mb drop in pressure, the sea level can be pulled up by 1 cm. Standard sea level air pressure is 1,013 mb. So, if a deep depression has a pressure of 960 mb at the centre, this will result in a sea level rise of about 50 cm.

As this 'dome' of water comes ashore, many factors can influence how damaging the storm surge is. For example, if it coincides with a high spring tide, the water levels will reach even further inland. Accompanying heavy rainfall can also exacerbate the effects of a storm surge and local geography comes into play, as water will flood a shallow coast more easily than a steep one. This was the case for one of the most infamous storm surges in history, brought by Hurricane Katrina. Coastal areas surrounding the Gulf of Mexico have a very shallow seabed and when Katrina hit in late August 2005, water inundated the coastal communities of Mississippi and Louisiana, with a storm surge of more than 8 metres in some areas. Almost the entire city of New Orleans was flooded as sea defences struggled to cope with the rising water.

Closer to home, the same principle is what led to the most destructive storm surge in recent history. On the night of 31 January 1953, a deep low-pressure system tracked southwards from the north-east of Scotland into the North Sea. It brought a 'dome' of deep water from the Atlantic and pushed it southwards into the relatively shallow North Sea. With the narrow English Channel essentially creating a bottleneck with nowhere for the water to go, coastal areas of Scotland, England, the Netherlands and Belgium experienced devastating floods. Sea levels rose by more than 6 metres above normal in some places. Around the North Sea coastline, more than 2,500 people lost their lives and 30,000 people were forced to leave their homes. It went down in history as one of the most destructive natural disasters in the UK. Keen to avoid a repetition of this devastating event, the UK government invested more money in sea defences along the east coast, including the Thames Barrier, which was officially opened in 1984 by Queen Elizabeth II.

The Thames Barrier, operational since 1982, is designed to protect London from North Sea storm surges.

The Beaufort Scale

Wind strength is commonly given on the Beaufort scale. This was originally defined by Francis Beaufort (later Admiral Beaufort) for use at sea, but was subsequently modified for use on land. Meteorologists generally specify the speed of the wind in metres per second (m s^{-1}). For wind speeds at sea, details are usually given in knots. The equivalents in kph are shown for speeds over land.

The Beaufort scale (for use at sea)

| Force | Description | Sea state | Speed | |
			Knots	m s^{-1}
0	calm	like a mirror	<1	0.0–0.2
1	light air	ripples, no foam	1–3	0.3–1.5
2	light breeze	small wavelets, smooth crests	4–6	1.6–3.3
3	gentle breeze	large wavelets, some crests break, a few white horses	7–10	3.4–5.4
4	moderate breeze	small waves, frequent white horses	11–16	5.5–7.9
5	fresh breeze	moderate, fairly long waves, many white horses, some spray	17–21	8.0–10.7
6	strong breeze	some large waves, extensive white foaming crests, some spray	22–27	10.8–13.8

The Beaufort scale (for use at sea) – *continued*

Force	Description	Sea state	Speed	
			Knots	m s⁻¹
7	near gale	sea heaping up, streaks of foam blowing in the wind	28–33	13.9–17.1
8	gale	fairly long and high waves, crests breaking into spindrift, foam in prominent streaks	34–40	17.2–20.7
9	strong gale	high waves, dense foam in wind, wave-crests topple and roll over, spray interferes with visibility	41–47	20.8–24.4
10	storm	very high waves with overhanging crests, dense blowing foam, sea appears white, heavy tumbling sea, poor visibility	48–55	24.5–28.4
11	violent storm	exceptionally high waves may hide small ships, sea covered in long, white patches of foam, waves blown into froth, poor visibility	56–63	28.5–32.6
12	hurricane	air filled with foam and spray, visibility extremely bad	64	32.7

The Beaufort scale (adapted for use on land)

Force	Description	Events on land	Speed km h⁻¹	m s⁻¹
0	calm	smoke rises vertically	<1	0.0–0.21
1	light air	direction of wind shown by smoke but not by wind vane	1–5	0.3–1.5
2	light breeze	wind felt on face, leaves rustle, wind vane turns to wind	6–11	1.6–3.3
3	gentle breeze	leaves and small twigs in motion, wind spreads small flags	12–19	3.4–5.4
4	moderate breeze	wind raises dust and loose paper, small branches move	20–29	5.5–7.9
5	fresh breeze	small leafy trees start to sway, wavelets with crests on inland waters	30–39	8.0–10.7
6	strong breeze	large branches in motion, whistling in telephone wires, difficult to use umbrellas	40–50	10.8–13.8
7	near gale	whole trees in motion, difficult to walk against wind	51–61	13.9–17.1

The Beaufort scale (adapted for use on land) – *continued*

Force	Description	Events on land	Speed km h⁻¹	m s⁻¹
8	gale	twigs break from trees, difficult to walk	62–74	17.2–20.7
9	strong gale	slight structural damage to buildings; chimney pots, tiles and aerials removed	75–87	20.8–24.4
10	storm	trees uprooted, considerable damage to buildings	88–101	24.5–28.4
11	violent storm	widespread damage to all types of building	102–117	28.5–32.6
12	hurricane	widespread destruction, only specially constructed buildings survive	$\geq$118	$\geq$32.7

The TORRO Tornado Scale

The TORRO tornado intensity scale is based on an extension to the Beaufort scale of wind speeds. The winds speeds are actually calculated mathematically from the accepted Beaufort wind speeds. (Although the Beaufort scale was first proposed in 1805, it was expressed in terms of wind speed in 1921.) T0 corresponds to Beaufort Force 8, and T11 would correspond to Beaufort Force 30 (if such a force existed).

The TORRO scale is thus solely based on wind speeds, unlike the Fujita scale and the later, modified version, the Enhanced Fujita scale, which are based on an assessment of damage. In practice, wind-speed measurements are rarely available for tornadoes, and so, in effect, both scales are, perforce, based on an assessment of the intensity of damage.

Scale	Wind speed (estimated)			Potential damage
	mph	km h⁻¹	m s⁻¹	
F0	0–38	0–60	0–16	**No damage.** *(Funnel cloud aloft, not a tornado)* No damage to structures, unless on tops of tallest towers, or to radiosondes, balloons and aircraft. No damage in the country, except possibly agitation to highest tree-tops and effect on birds and smoke. A whistling or rushing sound aloft may be noticed.
T0	39–54	61–86	17–24	**Light damage.** Loose light litter raised from ground-level in spirals. Tents, marquees seriously disturbed; most exposed tiles, slates on roofs dislodged. Twigs snapped; trail visible through crops.
T1	55–72	87–115	25–32	**Mild damage.** Deckchairs, small plants, heavy litter becomes airborne; minor damage to sheds. More serious dislodging of tiles, slates, chimney pots. Wooden fences flattened. Slight damage to hedges and trees.

The TORRO Tornado Scale – *continued*

| Scale | Wind speed (estimated) | | | Potential damage |
	mph	km h⁻¹	m s⁻¹	
T2	73–92	116–147	33–41	**Moderate damage.** Heavy mobile homes displaced, light caravans blown over, garden sheds destroyed, garage roofs torn away. Much damage to tiled roofs and chimney stacks. General damage to trees, some big branches twisted or snapped off, small trees uprooted.
T3	93–114	148–184	42–51	**Strong damage.** Mobile homes overturned / badly damaged; light caravans destroyed; garages and weak outbuildings destroyed; house roof timbers considerably exposed. Some larger trees snapped or uprooted.
T4	115–136	185–220	52–61	**Severe damage.** Motor cars levitated. Mobile homes airborne / destroyed; sheds airborne for considerable distances; entire roofs removed from some houses; roof timbers of stronger brick or stone houses completely exposed; gable ends torn away. Numerous trees uprooted or snapped.
T5	137–160	221–259	62–72	**Intense damage.** Heavy motor vehicles levitated; more serious building damage than for T4, yet house walls usually remaining; the oldest, weakest buildings may collapse completely.

The TORRO Tornado Scale – *continued*

Scale	Wind speed (estimated)			Potential damage
	mph	km h⁻¹	m s⁻¹	
T6	161–186	260–299	73–83	**Moderately-devastating damage.** Strongly built houses lose entire roofs and perhaps also a wall; windows broken on skyscrapers, more of the less-strong buildings collapse.
T7	187–212	300–342	84–95	**Strongly-devastating damage.** Wooden-frame houses wholly demolished; some walls of stone or brick houses beaten down or collapse; skyscrapers twisted; steel-framed warehouse-type constructions may buckle slightly. Locomotives thrown over. Noticeable debarking of trees by flying debris.
T8	213–240	343–385	96–107	**Severely-devastating damage.** Motor cars hurled great distances. Wooden-framed houses and their contents dispersed over long distances; stone or brick houses irreparably damaged; skyscrapers badly twisted and may show a visible lean to one side; shallowly anchored high rises may be toppled; other steel-framed buildings buckled.
T9	241–269	386–432	108–120	**Intensely-devastating damage.** Many steel-framed buildings badly damaged; skyscrapers toppled; locomotives or trains hurled some distances. Complete debarking of any standing tree-trunks.

The TORRO Tornado Scale – *continued*

Scale	Wind speed (estimated)			Potential damage
	mph	km h⁻¹	m s⁻¹	
T10	270–299	433–482	121–134	**Super damage.** Entire frame houses and similar buildings lifted bodily or completely from foundations and carried a large distance to disintegrate. Steel-reinforced concrete buildings may be severely damaged or almost obliterated.
T11	>300	>483	>135	**Phenomenal damage.** Strong framed, well-built houses leveled off foundations and swept away. Steel-reinforced concrete structures are completely destroyed. Tall buildings collapse. Some cars, trucks and train carriages may be thrown approximately 1 mile (1.6 kilometres).

TORRO Hailstorm Intensity Scale

The Tornado and Storm Research Organisation (TORRO) has not only developed a scale for rating tornadoes (see pages 252–255) but also one to judge the severity of hailstorm incidents. This scale is given in the following table, but it must be borne in mind that the severity of any hailstorm will depend (among other factors) upon the size of individual hailstones, their numbers and also the speed at which the storm itself travels across country.

Scale	Intensity	Hail size (mm)	Size comparison	Damage
H0	Hard hail	5–9	Pea	None
H1	Potentially damaging	10–15	Mothball	Slight general damage to plants, crops
H2	Significant	16–20	Marble, grape	Significant damage to fruit, crops, vegetation
H3	Severe	21–30	Walnut	Severe damage to fruit and crops Damage to glass and plastic structures Paint and wood scored
H4	Severe	31–40	Pigeon's egg > squash ball	Widespread damage to glass Damage to vehicle bodywork
H5	Destructive	41–50	Golf ball > pullet's egg	Wholesale destruction of glass Damage to tiled roofs Significant risk of injuries

TORRO Hailstorm Intensity Scale – *continued*

Scale	Intensity	Hail size (mm)	Size comparison	Damage
H6	Destructive	51–60	Hen's egg	Bodywork of grounded aircraft dented Brick walls pitted
H7	Destructive	61–75	Tennis ball > cricket ball	Severe roof damage Risk of serious injuries
H8	Destructive	76–90	Large orange > softball	Severe damage to aircraft bodywork
H9	Super hailstorms	91–100	Grapefruit	Extensive structural damage
H10	Super hailstorms	>100	Melon	Extensive structural damage Risk of severe or fatal injuries to persons caught in the open

Twilight Diagrams

Sunrise, sunset, twilight

For each individual month, we give details of sunrise and sunset times for the four capital cities of the various countries that make up the United Kingdom.

During the summer, especialy at high latitudes, twilight may persist throughout the night and make it difficult to see the faintest stars. Beyond the Arctic and Antarctic Circles, of course, the Sun does not set for 24 hours at least once during the summer (and rise for 24 hours at least once during the winter). Even when the Sun does dip below the horizon at high latitudes, bright twilight persists throughout the night, so observing the fainter stars is impossible. Even in Britain this applies to northern Scotland, which is why we include a diagram for Lerwick in the Shetland Islands.

As mentioned earlier (page 11) there are three recognised stages of twilight: civil twilight, nautical twilight and astronomical twilight. Full darkness occurs only when the Sun is more than 18° below the horizon. During nautical twilight, only the very brightest stars are visible. During astronmical twilight, the faintest stars visible to the naked eye may be seen directly overhead, but are lost at lower altitudes. They become visible only once it is fully dark. The diagrams show the duration of twilight at the various locations. Of the locations shown, during the summer months there is astronomical twilight for a short time at Belfast, and this lasts longer during the summer at all of the other locations. To illustrate the way in which twilight occurs in the far south of Britain, we include a diagram showing twilight duration at St Mary's in the Scilly Isles. (A similar situation applies to the Channel Islands, which are also in the far south.) Once again, full darkness never occurs.

The diagrams show the times of New and Full Moon (black and white symbols, respectively). As may be seen, at most locations during the year roughly half of New and Full Moon phases may come during daylight. For this reason, the exact phase may be invisible in Britain, but be clearly seen elsewhere in the world. The exact times of the events are given in the diagrams for each individual month.

Lerwick, Shetland Islands – Latitude 60.2°N – Longitude 1.1°W

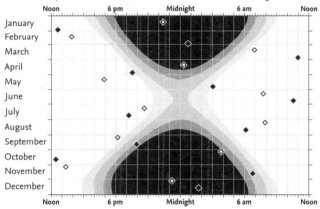

Edinburgh, UK – Latitude 55.9°N – Longitude 3.2°W

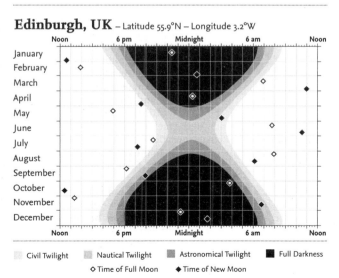

Civil Twilight Nautical Twilight Astronomical Twilight Full Darkness

◇ Time of Full Moon ◆ Time of New Moon

Belfast, UK – Latitude 54.6°N – Longitude 5.8°W

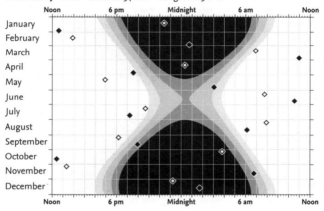

Cardiff, UK – Latitude 51.5°N – Longitude 3.2°W

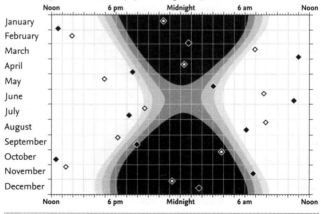

Civil Twilight   Nautical Twilight   Astronomical Twilight   Full Darkness

◇ Time of Full Moon   ◆ Time of New Moon

London, UK – Latitude 51.5°N – Longitude 2.0°W

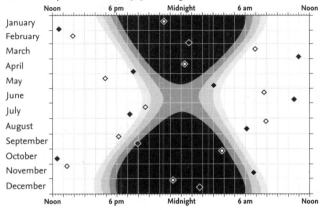

St Mary's, Scilly Isles – Latitude 49.9°N – Longitude 6.4°W

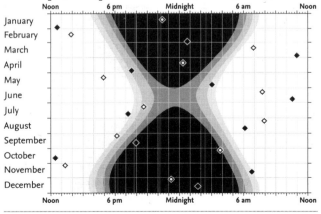

Civil Twilight   Nautical Twilight   Astronomical Twilight   Full Darkness
◇ Time of Full Moon   ◆ Time of New Moon

Further Reading and Internet Links

Books

Chaboud, René, *How Weather Works* (Thames & Hudson, 1996)

Dunlop, Storm, *Clouds* (Haynes, 2018)

Dunlop, Storm, *Collins Gem Weather* (HarperCollins, 1999)

Dunlop, Storm, *Collins Nature Guide Weather* (HarperCollins, 2004)

Dunlop, Storm, *Come Rain or Shine* (Summersdale, 2011)

Dunlop, Storm, *Dictionary of Weather* (2nd edition, Oxford University Press, 2008)

Dunlop, Storm, *Guide to Weather Forecasting* (rev. printing, Philip's, 2013)

Dunlop, Storm, *How to Identify Weather* (HarperCollins, 2002)

Dunlop, Storm, *How to Read the Weather* (Pavilion, 2018)

Dunlop, Storm, *Weather* (Cassell Illustrated, 2006/2007)

Eden, Philip, *Weatherwise* (Macmillan, 1995)

File, Dick, *Weather Facts*, (Oxford University Press, 1996)

Hamblyn, Richard & Meteorological Office, *The Cloud Book: How to Understand the Skies* (David & Charles, 2009)

Hamblyn, Richard & Meteorological Office, *Extraordinary Clouds* (David & Charles, 2009)

Kington, John, *Climate and Weather* (HarperCollins, 2010)

Ludlum, David, *Collins Wildlife Trust Guide Weather* (HarperCollins, 2001)

Meteorological Office, *Cloud Types for Observers* (HMSO, 1982)

Met Office, Factsheets 1–19 (pdfs downloadable from: http://www.metoffice.gov.uk/learning/library/publications/factsheets)

Watts, Alan, *Instant Weather Forecasting* (Adlard Coles Nautical, 2000)

Watts, Alan, *Instant Wind Forecasting* (Adlard Coles Nautical, 2001)

Watts, Alan, *The Weather Handbook* (3rd edn, Adlard Coles Nautical, 2014)

Whitaker, Richard, ed., *Weather: The Ultimate Guide to the Elements* (HarperCollins, 1996)

Williams, Jack, *The AMS Weather Book: The Ultimate Guide to America's Weather* (Univ. Chicago Press, 2009)

Woodward, A., & Penn, R., *The Wrong Kind of Snow* (Hodder & Stoughton, 2007)

Internet links – Current weather

AccuWeather: *http://www.accuweather.com/*
      UK: *http://www.accuweather.com/ukie/index.asp?*

Australian Weather News:
    http://www.australianweathernews.com/

    UK station plots:
        http://www.australianweathernews.com/sitepages/
        charts/611_United_Kingdom.shtml

BBC Weather: *http://www.bbc.co.uk/weather*

CNN Weather: *http://www.cnn.com/WEATHER/index.html*

Intellicast: *http://intellicast.com/*

ITV Weather: *http://www.itv-weather.co.uk/*

Unisys Weather: *http://weather.unisys.com/*

UK Met Office: *http://www.metoffice.gov.uk*

    Forecasts:
        *http://www.metoffice.gov.uk/weather/uk/uk_forecast_*
        weather.html

    Hourly weather data:
        http://www.metoffice.gov.uk/education/teachers/
        latest-weather-data-uk

    Latest station plot:
        http://www.metoffice.gov.uk/data/education/chart_latest.gif

    Surface pressure charts:
        http://www.metoffice.gov.uk/public/weather/surface-pressure/

    Explanation of symbols on pressure charts:
        http://www.metoffice.gov.uk/guide/weather/
        symbols#pressure-symbols

    Synoptic & climate stations (interactive map):
        http://www.metoffice.gov.uk/public/weather/climate-network/
        #?tab=climateNetwork

Weather Underground:
    http://www.wunderground.com

Wetter3 (German site with global information):
    http://www.wetter3.de

    UK Met Office chart archive:
        http://www.wetter3.de/Archiv/archiv_ukmet.html

General information

Atmospheric Optics:
http://www.atoptics.co.uk/

Hurricane Zone Net:
http://www.hurricanezone.net/

National Climate Data Centre:
http://www.ncdc.noaa.gov/

Extremes:
http://www.ncdc.noaa.gov/oa/climate/severeweather/extremes.html

National Hurricane Center:
http://www.nhc.noaa.gov/

Reading University (Roger Brugge):
http://www.met.reading.ac.uk/~brugge/index.html

UK Weather Information:
http://www.weather.org.uk/

WorldClimate:
http://www.worldclimate.com/

Meteorological Offices, Agencies and Organisations

Environment Canada:
http://www.msc-smc.ec.gc.ca/

European Centre for Medium-Range Weather Forecasting (ECMWF):
http://www.ecmwf.int

European Meteorological Satellite Organisation:
http://www.eumetsat.int/website/home/index.html

Intergovernmental Panel on Climate Change:
http://www.ipcc.ch

National Oceanic and Atmospheric Administration (NOAA):
http://www.noaa.gov/

National Weather Service (NWS):
http://www.nws.noaa.gov/

UK Meteorological Office:
http://www.metoffice.gov.uk

World Meteorological Organisation:
http://www.wmo.int

Satellite images

Eumetsat:
http://www.eumetsat.de/

Image library:
http://www.eumetsat.int/website/home/Images/ImageLibrary/index.html

Group for Earth Observation (GEO):
http://www.geo-web.org.uk/

Societies

American Meteorological Society:
http://www.ametsoc.org/AMS

Australian Meteorological and Oceanographic Society:
http://www.amos.org.au

Canadian Meteorological and Oceanographic Society:
http://www.cmos.ca/

European Meteorological Society:
http://www.emetsoc.org/

Irish Meteorological Society:
http://www.irishmetsociety.org

National Weather Association, USA:
http://www.nwas.org/

New Zealand Meteorological Society:
http://www.metsoc.org.nz/

Royal Meteorological Society:
http://www.rmets.org

TORRO: Hurricanes and Storm Research Organisation:
http://torro.org.uk

Acknowledgements

Index